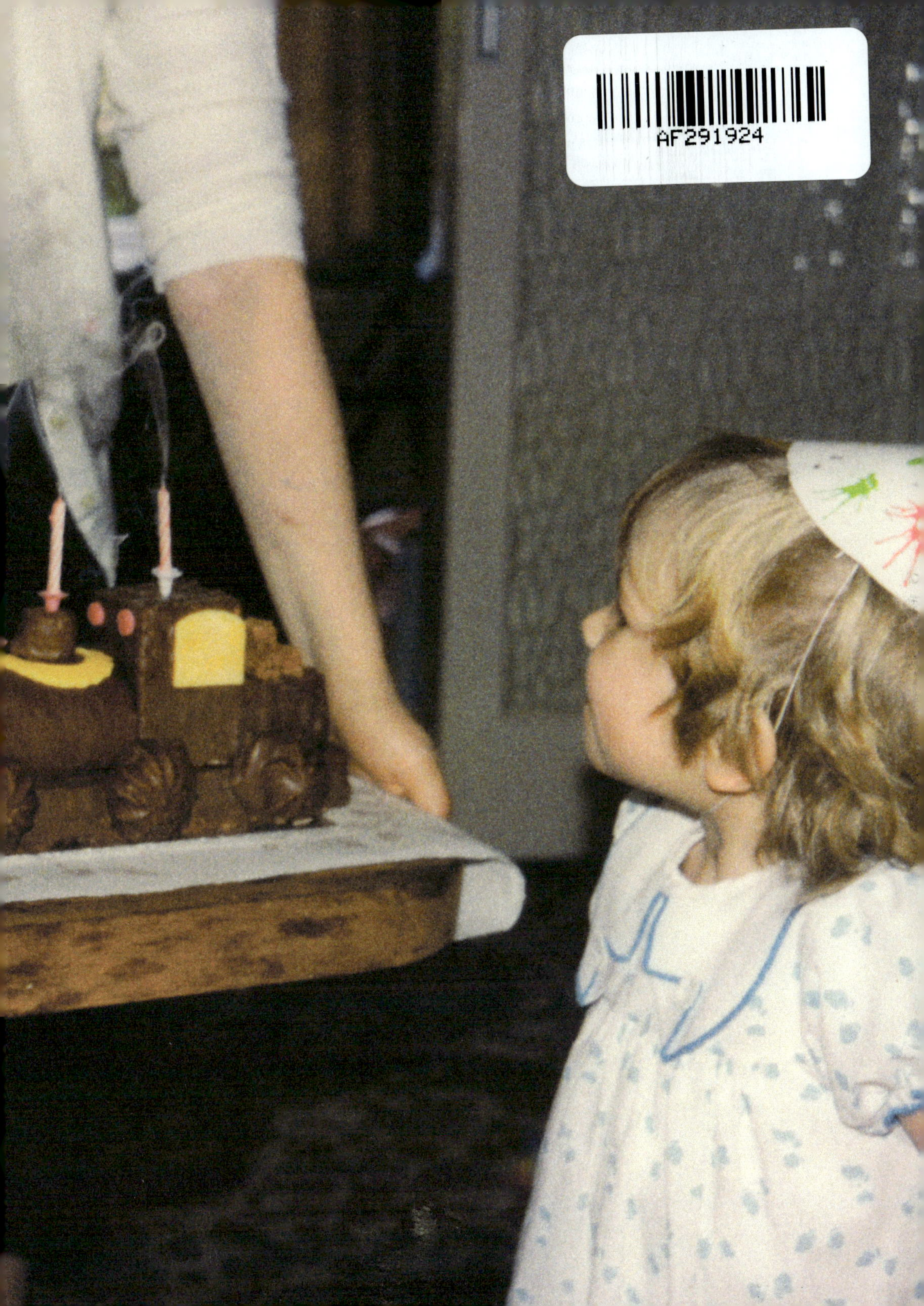

AF291924

More Than A Snapshot
A Visual History of Photo Wallets

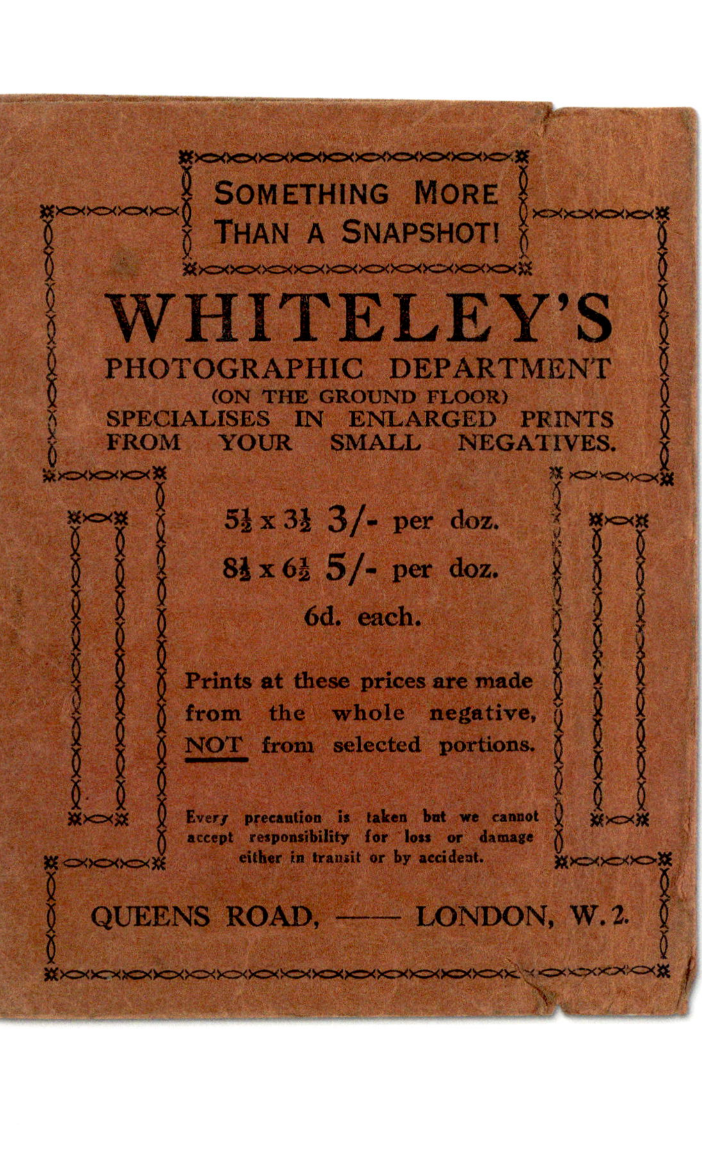

More Than A Snapshot
A Visual History of Photo Wallets

Annebella Pollen

Four Corners Irregulars
Nº 10

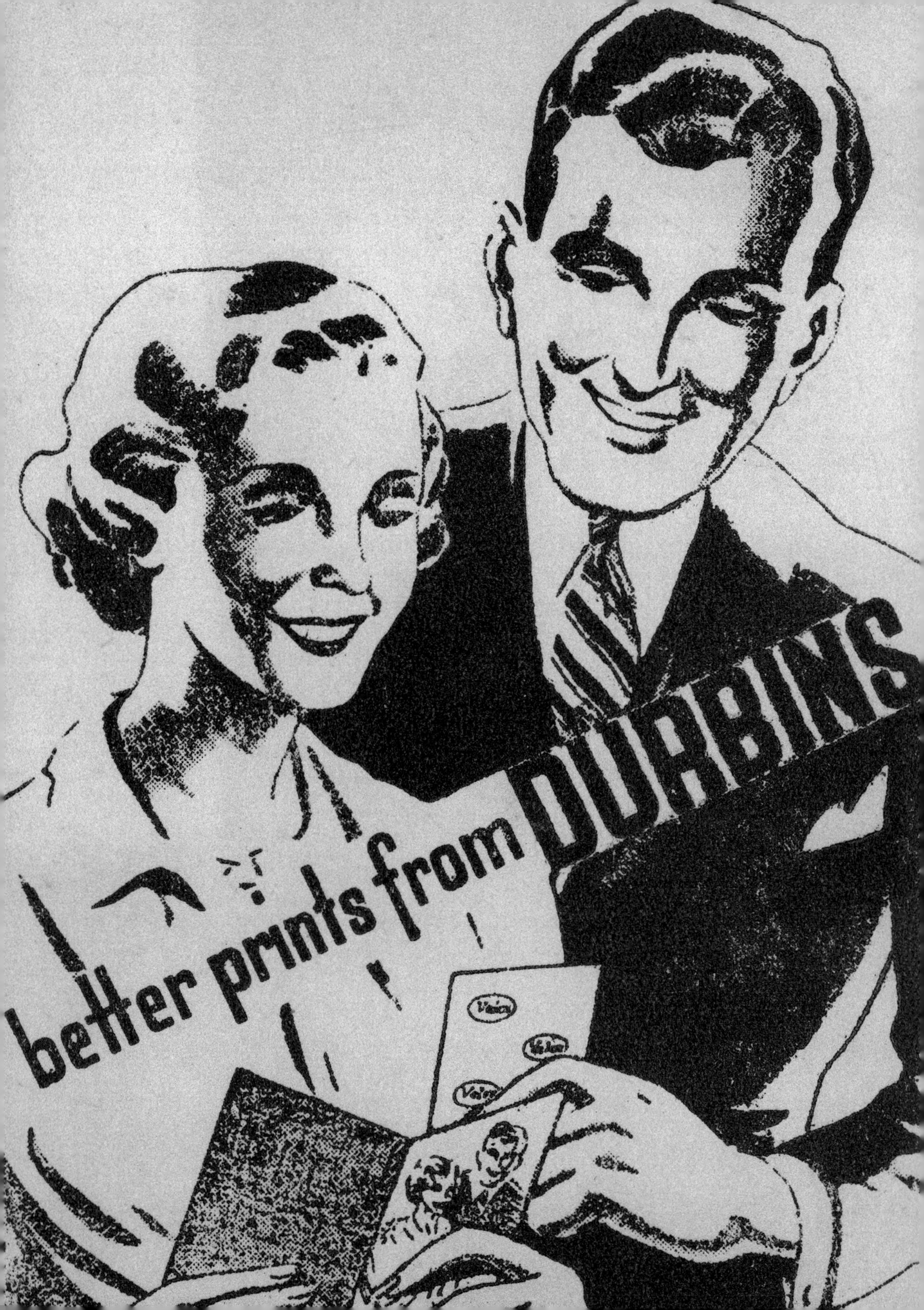

better prints from DURBINS

Contents

Photo Wallet

Taking the Picture Is Only the First Step

Across the land, photographic print wallets are stacked in biscuit tins and shoe boxes, stored in attics and tucked under beds. These paper envelopes, containing negatives and prints not good enough for the family album, were a once-practical means for commercial photographic developers to return prints to customers when they had their films processed. Usually overlooked as cultural objects in their own right, these humble items might seem to be of lesser importance than the photographs they hold. Yet, for around a hundred years, print wallets communicated photographic ideals and promoted products, provided advice and modelled behaviour. Seen together, their striking graphic styles and imaginative advertising messages show a photographic world of technologies, companies and services mostly lost in our digital present.

Kodak announced the introduction of what they called 'print wallets' in 1908, as 'a neat double envelope with one side designed to hold photographs and the other negatives.'[1] Also referred to as 'film wallets' and 'photo wallets' – if formally named at all – these simple paper folders offer an alternative history of popular photographic practice. Rich with imagery, mostly by anonymous illustrators and photographers, and with texts that convey photographic expectations and sustain social norms, they communicate in confined spaces with a striking economy of means. They show what subjects are considered photographable, and they reinforce prohibitions by what they omit. As print wallets shift in style and scale, over a century of photographic change, their cheap buff paper develops into glossy full colour. They map growing camera ownership in Britain and the services that supported it, and they chart, one hundred years on, the decline of commercial film processing as a mass form.

All the wallets in this book are from my own collection of many hundreds of examples, built up over more than a decade of rummaging at bric-a-brac stalls and car boot sales. I rarely spend more than a pound or two and many wallets I have received free from dealers employed in end-of-life house clearances. They are battered and bruised examples rather

Opposite: A plain-spoken photo wallet, 1920s.

than pristine specimens. Although the common definition of printed ephemera – of which print wallets are a part – is that they are 'the minor transient documents of everyday life', these endure.[2] They have been well-thumbed over lifetimes, and some carry their former owners' annotations, signalling the subjects of the prints that they once contained ('American cousins' or 'Dudley Zoo'), recording holiday destinations (Bognor to Egypt), and they sometimes come with apologetic requests for reprints or photographers' evaluations of their contents ('Boring'). Those in my collection are emptied of their photographs and isolated from their origins, but their scuffs and scrawls inscribe prices and dates, journeys and relationships over popular photography's public image of happy families and beautiful views. They sometimes reveal a differing set of values and practices than those instructed by the manufacturers.

Opposite and preceding pages: Whether branded or plain, advertising
local suppliers or international manufacturers, and illustrated with
drawings or photographs, the photo wallet endured for more
than a century as a folded envelope containing prints and negatives.

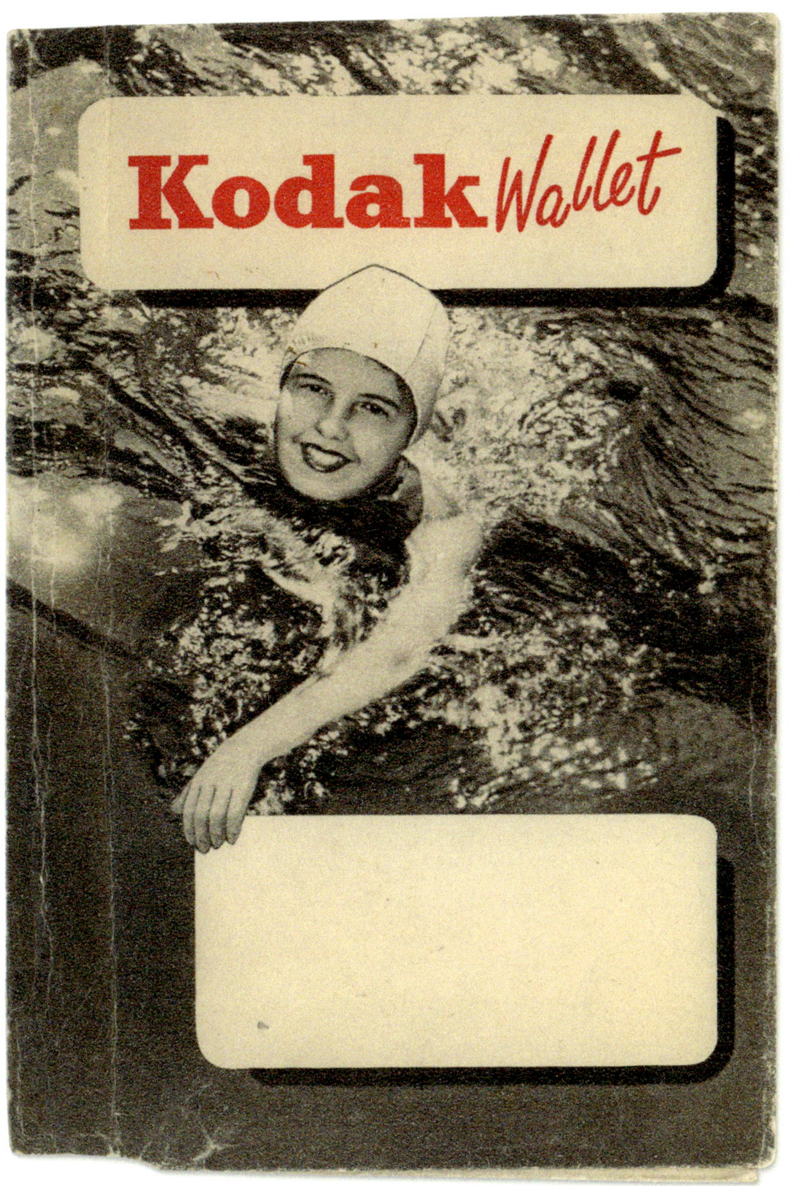

Kodak Wallet

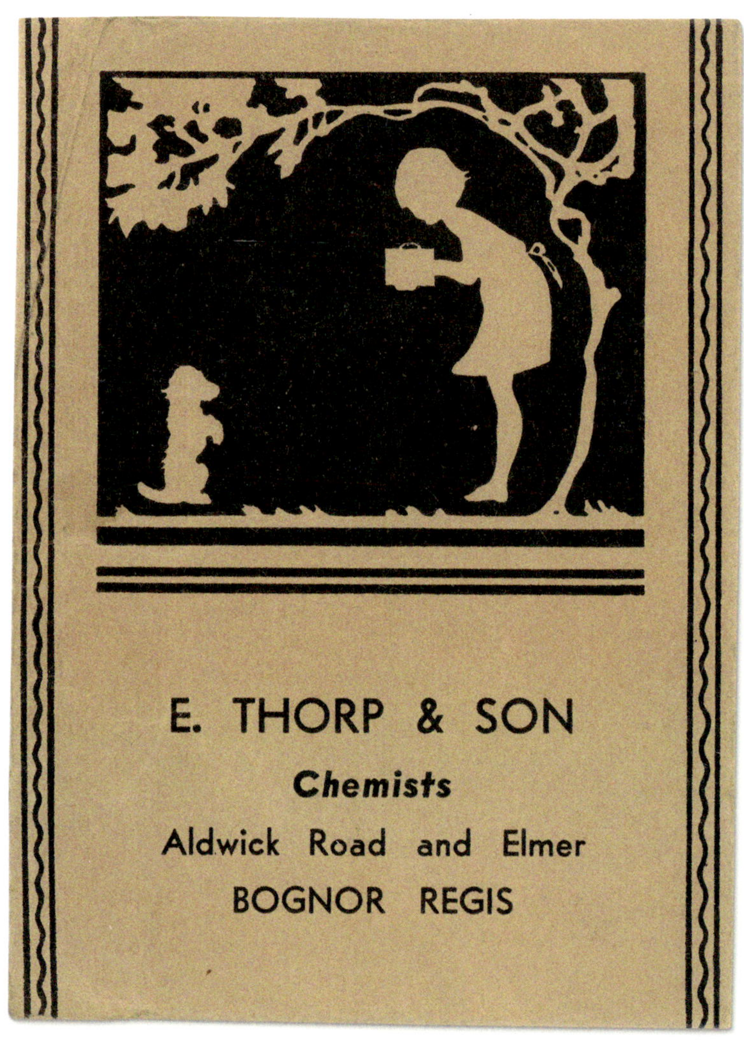

Early wallets often illustrated photographic practices using non-photographic techniques, from line drawings to silhouettes. Children using cameras showed photography's simplicity, c.1930s.

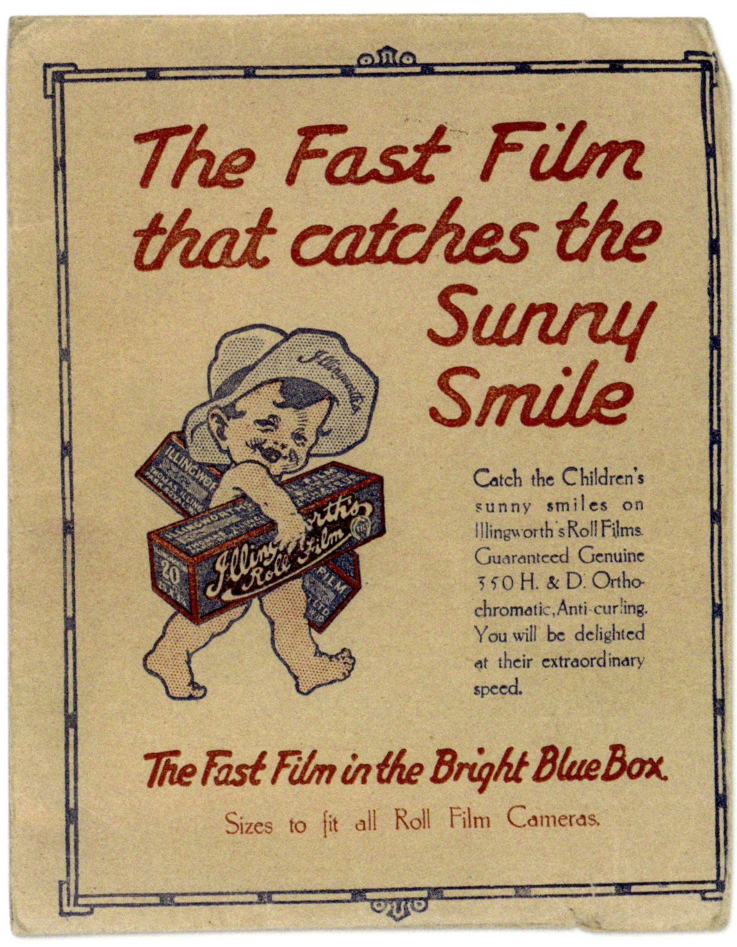

Advertising characters – such as Illingworth's toddler,
dressed only in a sunhat, carrying outsize boxes of film –
modelled suitable subjects of happy families and sunny days, c.1920s.

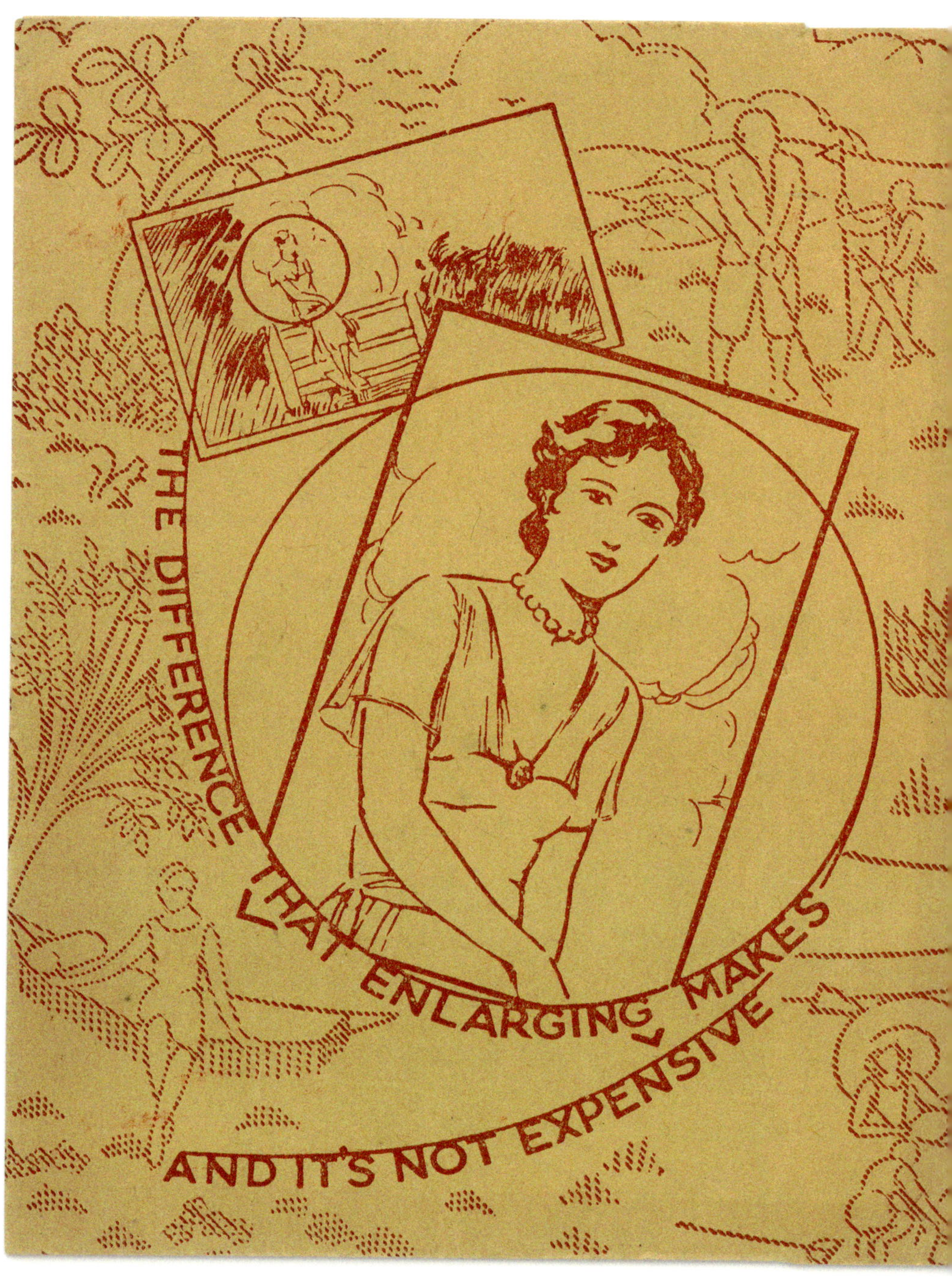

The young woman on this interwar wallet is both photographer and subject.
The pointillist scenes show photography's links to leisure: motoring and cycling,
golf and fishing, picnics and hammocks.

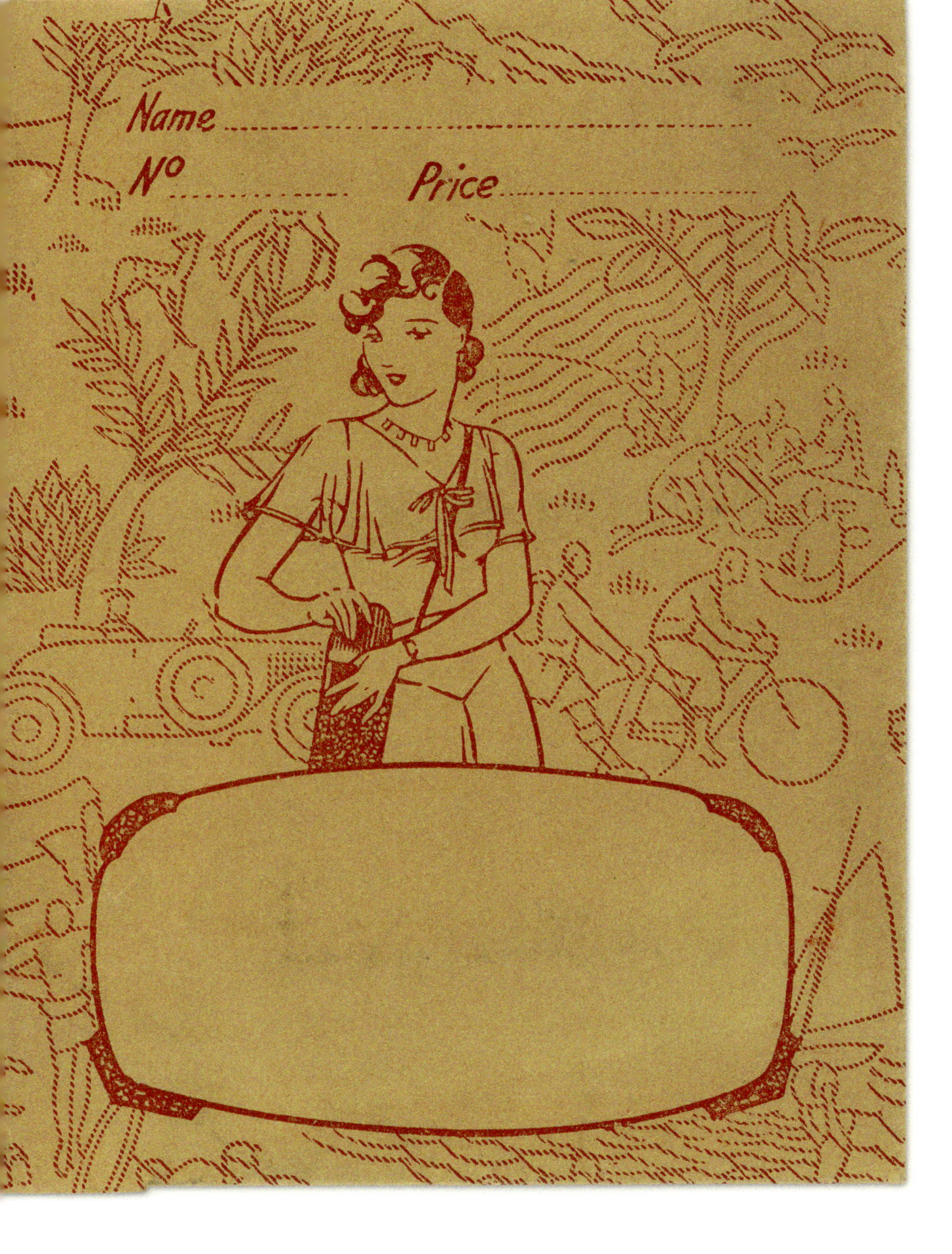

Name
Nº
Price

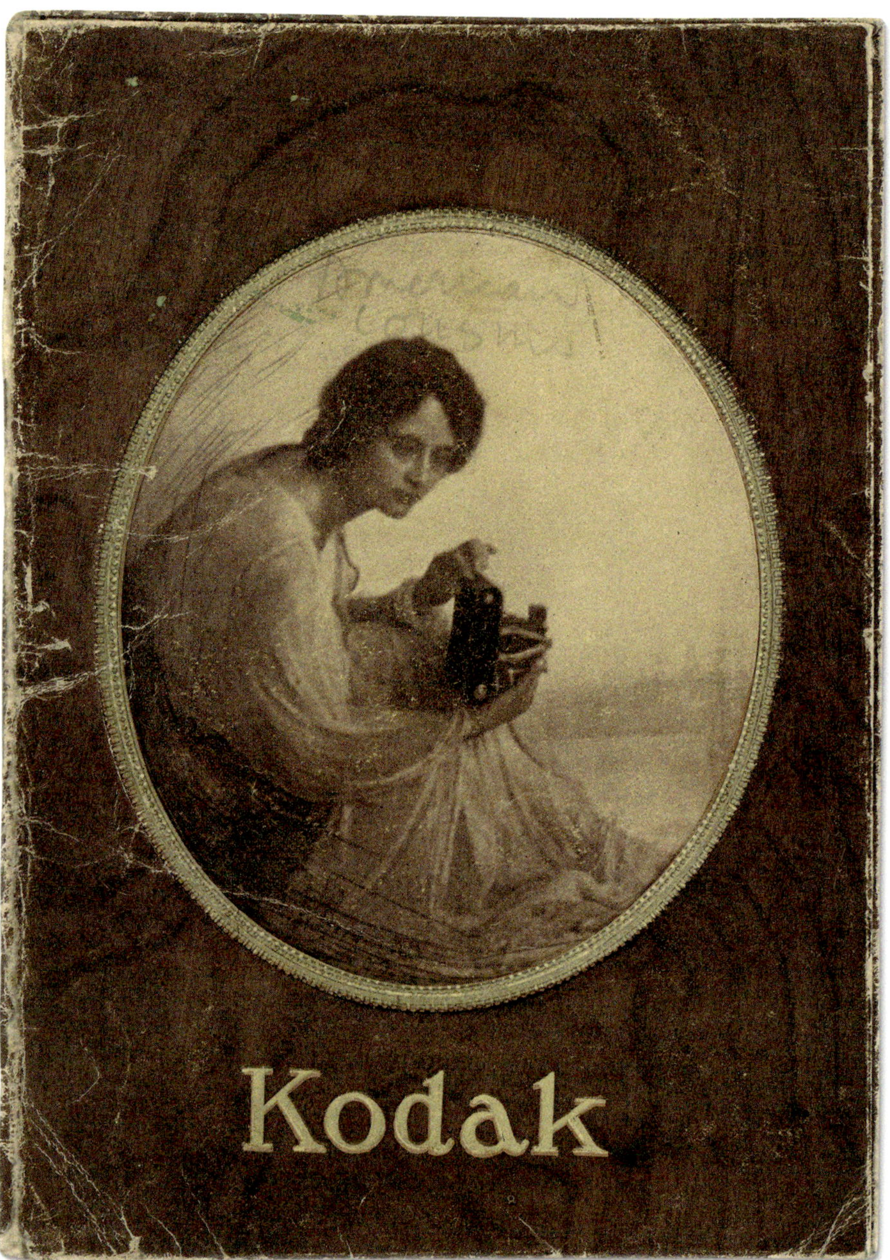

Kodak

The Latest Bit of Kodak's Wizardry

The first fifty years of photographic production required complex and cumbersome equipment and processes that put the practice beyond those without the requisite income, training or time. Under the Kodak brand in North America in the late 1880s, inventor George Eastman created simple-to-operate cameras, preloaded with film to be sent away for processing. Kodak's simplified products and services – especially as they became more affordable at the start of the twentieth century – ensured that photography appealed to the widest range of users, including those with no technical enthusiasm or artistic ambition, and no darkroom. Kodak made snapshot photography into an accessible single-gesture action, and their enormous advertising programme promoted it particularly to women and children. For a modest fee, and following a short wait of a few days, hundreds of thousands of new photographers could exchange exposed films at their local chemists or camera retailers for black and white prints wrapped in an informative, attractive wallet.

Kodak print wallets used in Britain before the end of the First World War were styled to mimic existing, luxurious photographic presentations, such as picture frames, with paper swirled to resemble wood grain and embossed gold borders, or photograph albums, with imitation leather patterns and an oval aperture like a pre-cut slot on an album page. These examples carried through imagery used on Kodak catalogues, aligning processing services with the wider universe of Kodak products – cameras, accessories, tools and apparatus – many of which were also promoted for sale on wallets' inner folds. Early wallets showed women and girls, cameras in hand, in white dresses amid sepia-toned pastoral settings. Kodak did not always credit those who provided their wallet imagery, but photographs were sourced through competitions promoted in their magazines and illustrations were commissioned from professionals on both sides of the Atlantic.[3]

The earliest envelope in my collection features a photograph by the American artist Anne Brigman, which was used on the 1908 Kodak

Opposite: Anne Brigman's *The Spirit of Photography* was used on Kodak catalogues and wallets from 1908. The former owner of this wallet labelled its contents: 'American Cousins'.

catalogue. It depicts an unknown sitter in a misty landscape, produced in a soft painterly style, and is an adaptation of Brigman's print, *The Spirit of Photography*, which showed the same sitter capturing a bubble with her camera as a symbol of photographic evanescence. Brigman used family and friends as models, transforming them into allegorical figures. Its subject is simultaneously an independent New Woman in possession of the latest gadget and an ancient Greek goddess in a diaphanous gown. Brigman first picked up a camera in 1901, attracted by Kodak's appeal to female photographers but, ironically for an image used to promote the company, she turned away from snapshots and became committed to Pictorialism, a photographic style that emphasised expression, atmosphere and the production of fine prints. *The Spirit of Photography* was platinum printed. The process provided tonal range, and Brigman added pencilled details to secure its artistic hand-drawn status.[4] Customers using Kodak's cheap cameras and commercial processing services were unlikely to get prints that looked like Brigman's but, before the bubble burst, her lead set a lofty mood. On the back of the wallet, Kodak advertised their London shops. Inside, they advised on flower and pet photography and explained that 'charming' enlargements made suitably decorative gifts for friends.

These sentimental and relational emphases, and the central depiction of women, helped compound Kodak's positioning of snapshot photography as a feminine pastime and responsibility. Female subjects appeared in white to suggest the cleanliness of photography when separated from the messiness of the darkroom; portable cameras were carried on straps as if fashion accessories. In 1910, Kodak introduced a distinctive blue-and-white striped dress for the brand character who would appear on their print wallets and posters for the next fifty years or so. The carefree, out-doorsy and well-off Kodak Girl climbed cliffs, drove motor cars and even travelled on skis with a camera at her side. Drawn by some of the leading British illustrators of the early twentieth century, including Fred Pegram, Claude Shepperton and A. Wallis Mills, she proved remarkably adaptable even as the cut of her dress followed the vagaries of fashion. Her hairstyles moved through shingled bob to blow-and-set, and her cameras moved from boxes and bellows at waist height to eye-level devices. Kodak's modern girl with a modern tool was a model to look at and to learn from. She smilingly demonstrated how to hold a camera, gently reinforced what subjects were photographically fitting, and she pointed elegantly at prizes to be won in snapshot competitions.[5]

Opposite: Early Kodak wallets included textured finishes imitating wood grain and leather, with oval apertures resembling the form of picture frames and photograph albums, c.1910s.

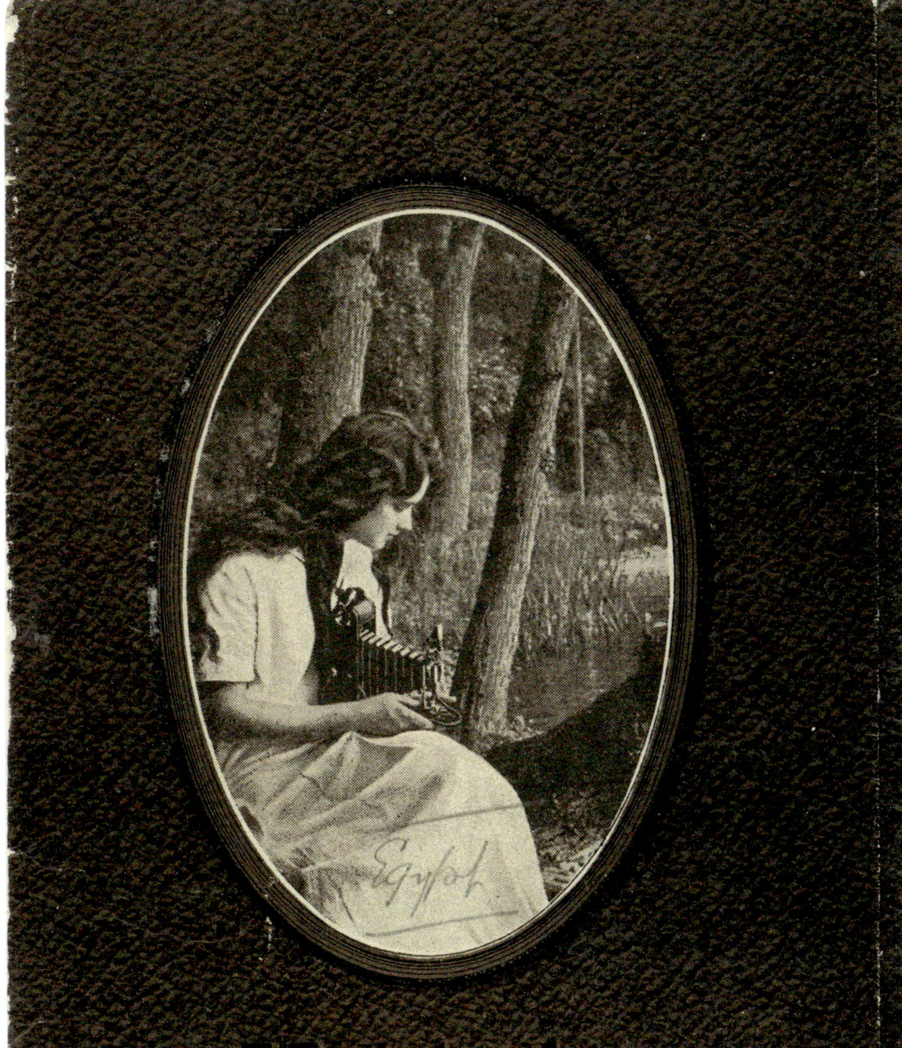

Kodak

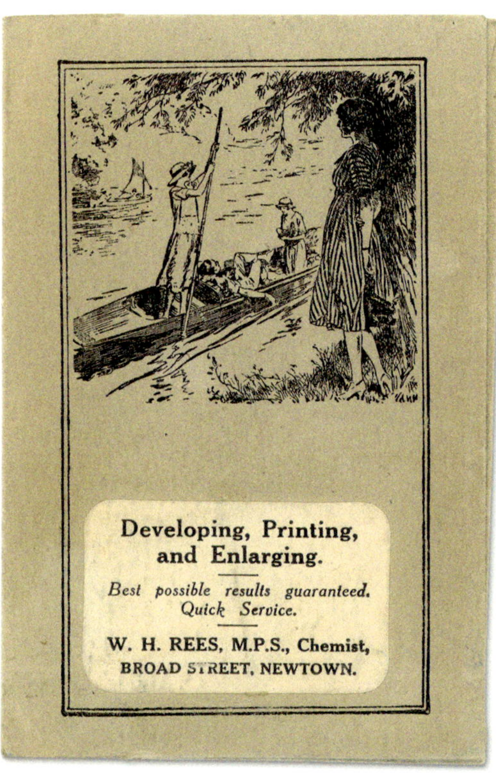

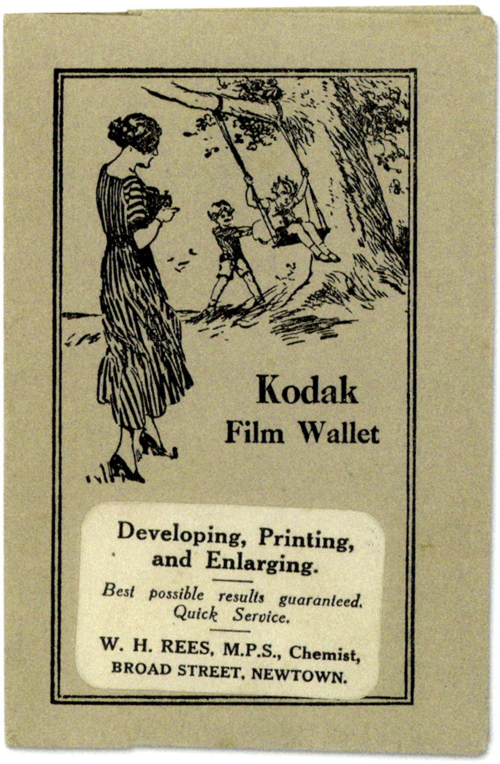

The fashionable Kodak Girl character, often clad in a striped dress, was depicted by leading illustrators in the act of snapping her friends and family in breezy outdoor settings in the 1920s.

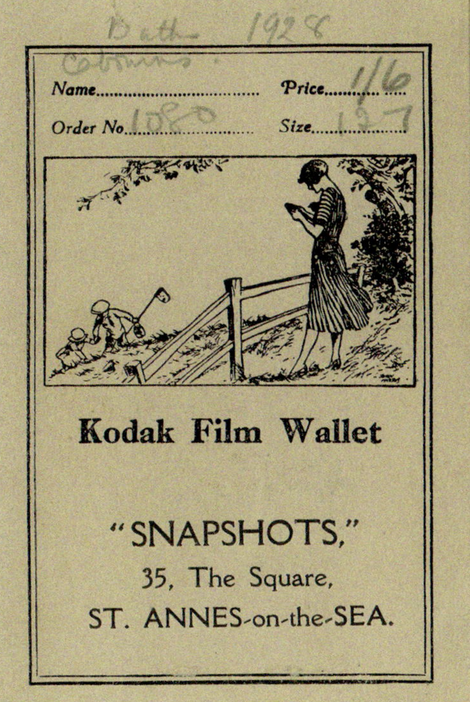

Kodak Film Wallet

"SNAPSHOTS,"
35, The Square,
ST. ANNES-on-the-SEA.

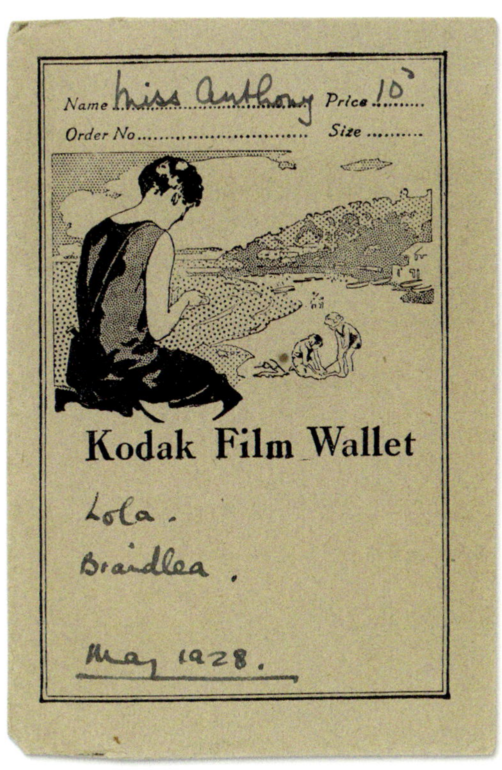

Kodak Film Wallet

NAME......*Mrs Hopkins*......

ORDER Nº.........................

SIZE............................

SPOOLS.........................

PRINTS.........................

ENLGTS.........................

PRICE..........................

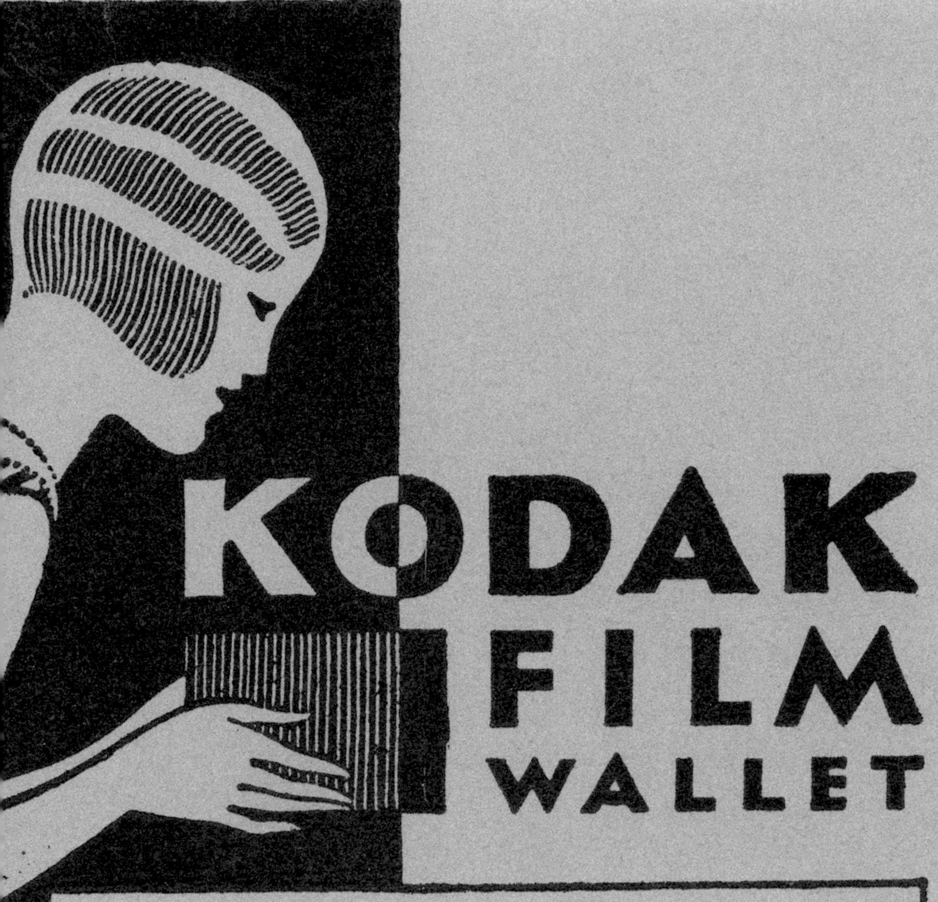
KODAK
FILM
WALLET

C. H. ROBINS, M.P.S.,
Photographic Chemist,
The Kensey Vale Pharmacy,
LAUNCESTON.
Telephone No. 125.

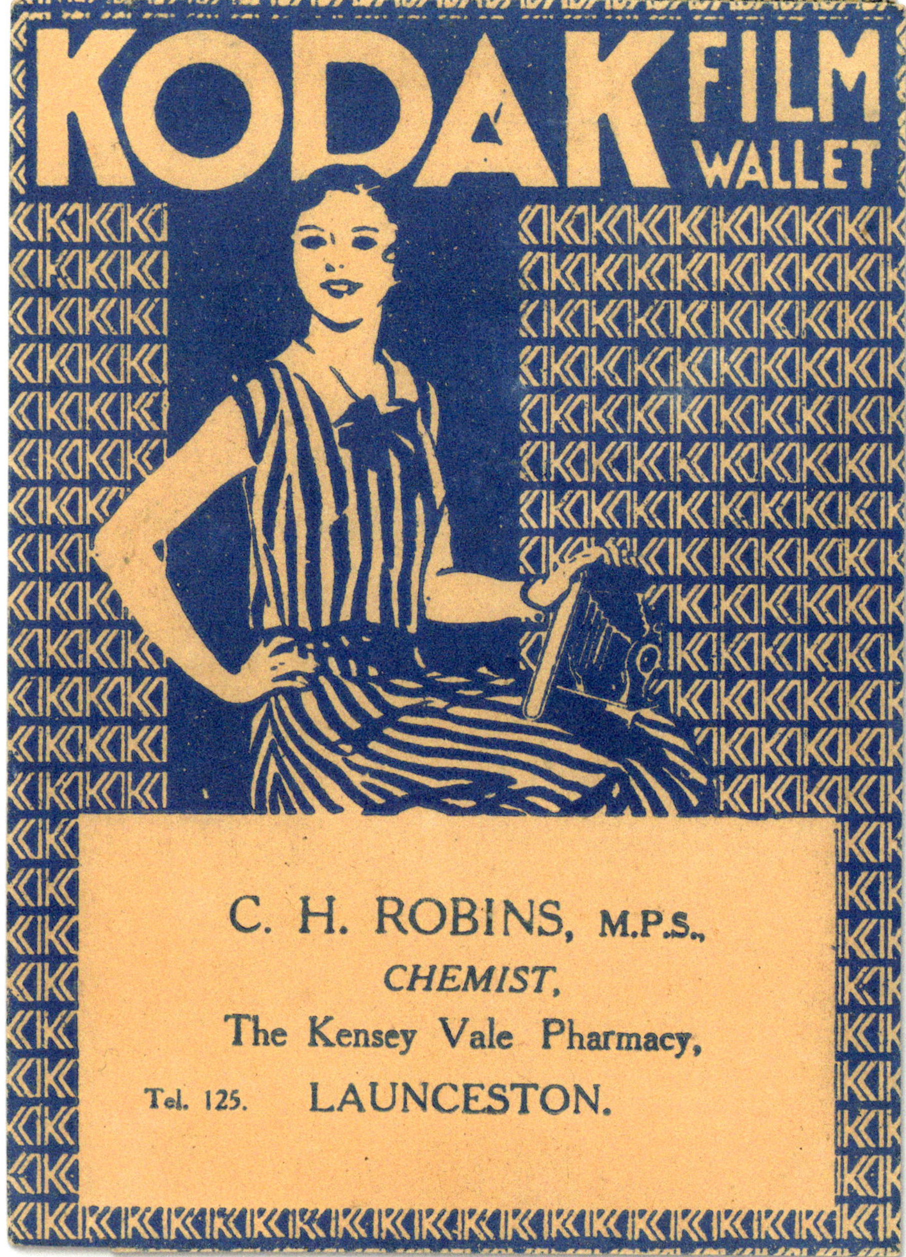

KODAK FILM WALLET
C. H. ROBINS, M.P.S.,
CHEMIST,
The Kensey Vale Pharmacy,
Tel. 125.   LAUNCESTON.

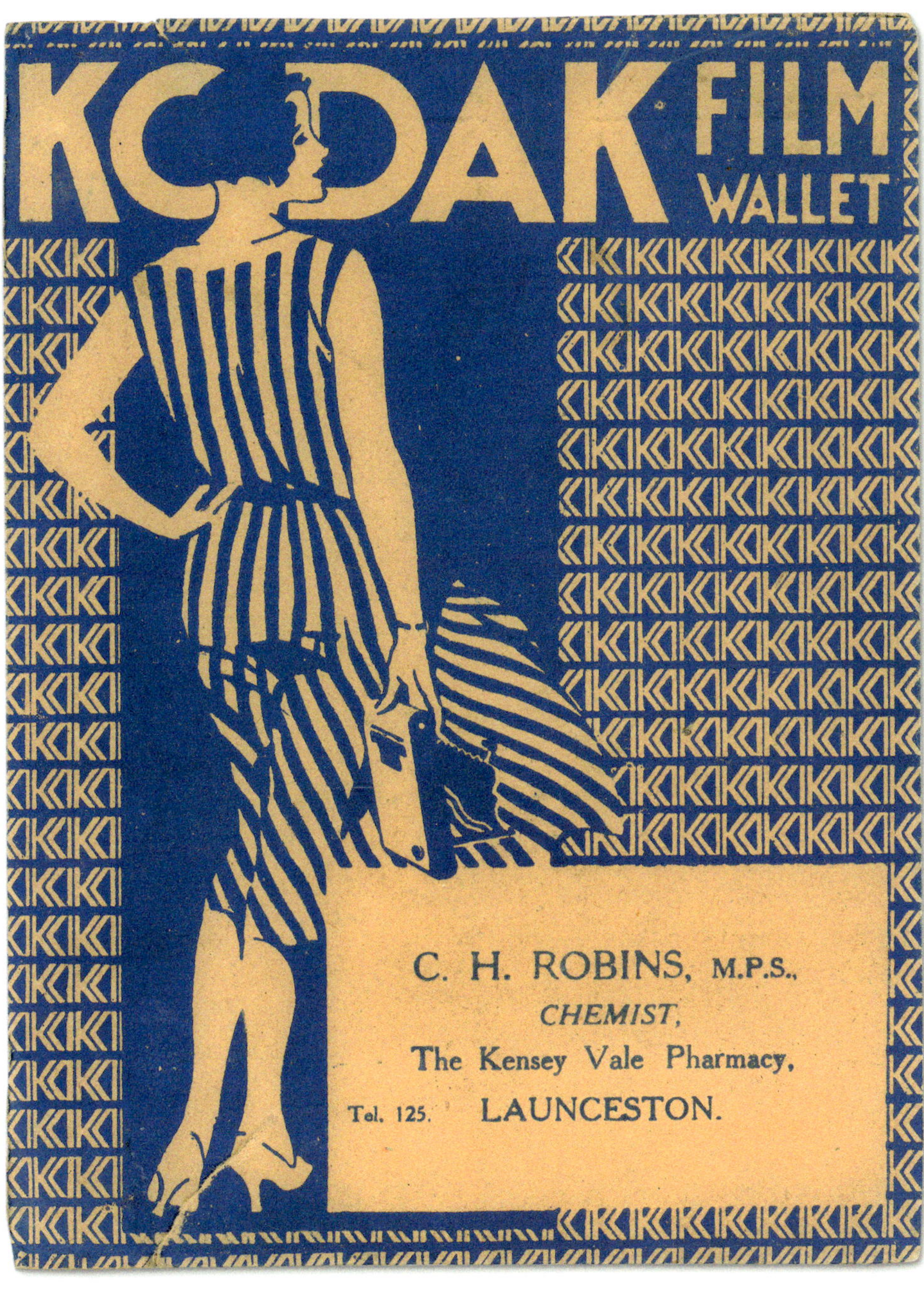

KODAK FILM WALLET
C. H. ROBINS, M.P.S.,
CHEMIST,
The Kensey Vale Pharmacy,
Tel. 125. LAUNCESTON.

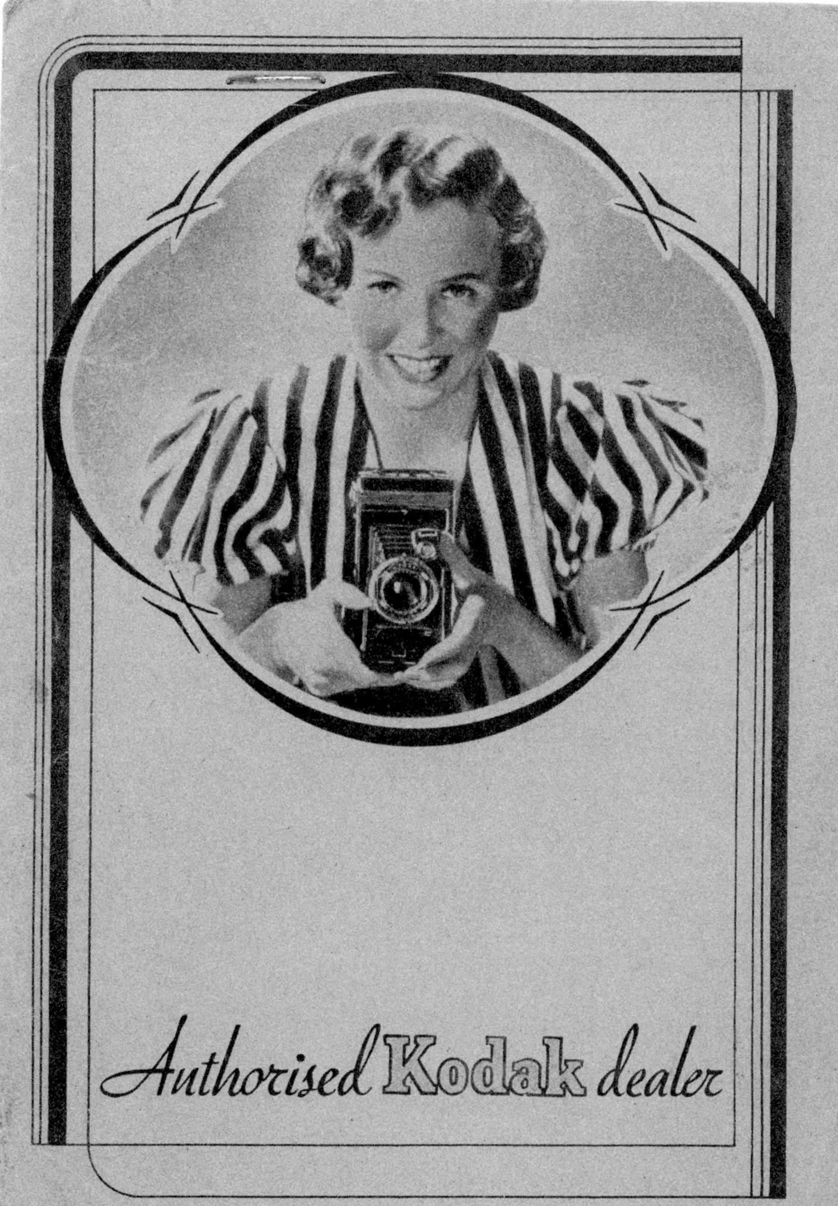
Authorised Kodak dealer

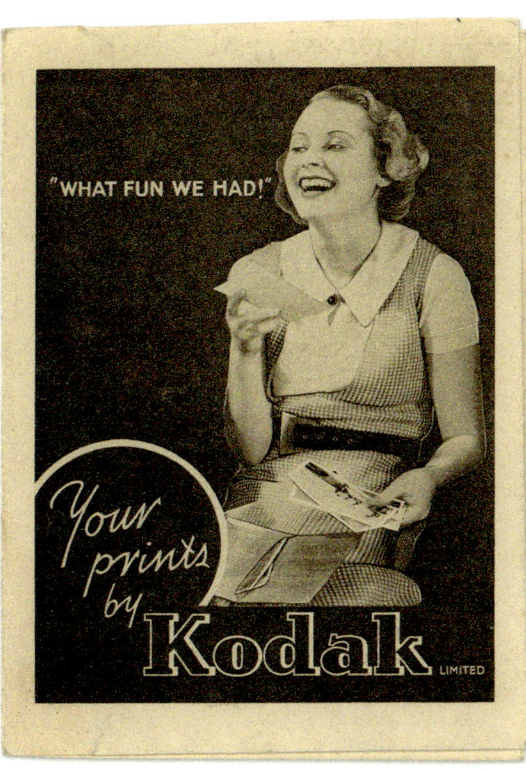

"WHAT FUN WE HAD!"
Your prints by
Kodak
LIMITED

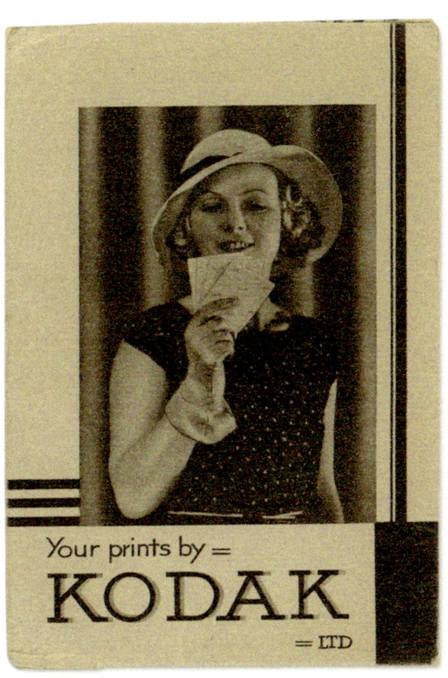

Your prints by =
KODAK
= LTD

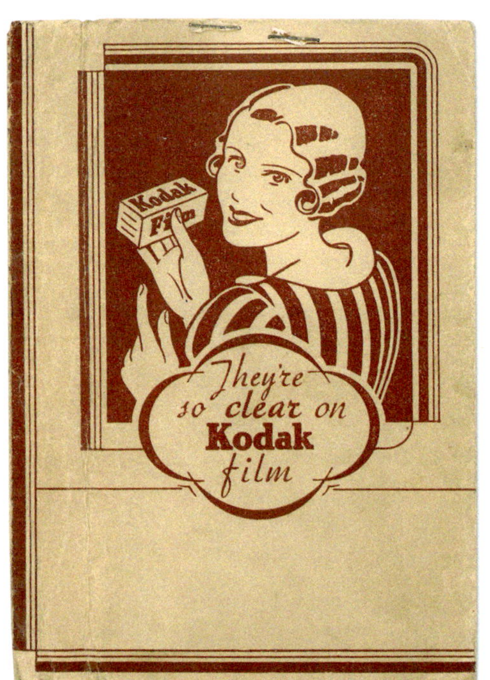
Kodak
Film
They're
so clear on
Kodak
film

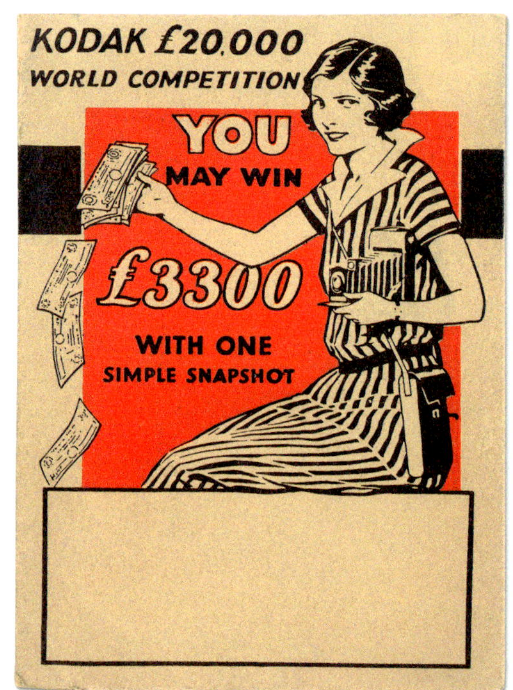
KODAK £20,000
WORLD COMPETITION
YOU
MAY WIN
£3300
WITH ONE
SIMPLE SNAPSHOT

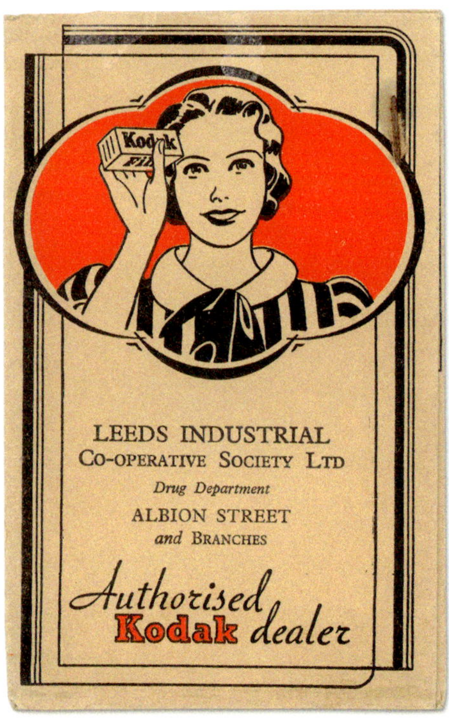
Kodak
Film
LEEDS INDUSTRIAL
Co-operative Society Ltd
Drug Department
ALBION STREET
and Branches
Authorised
Kodak dealer

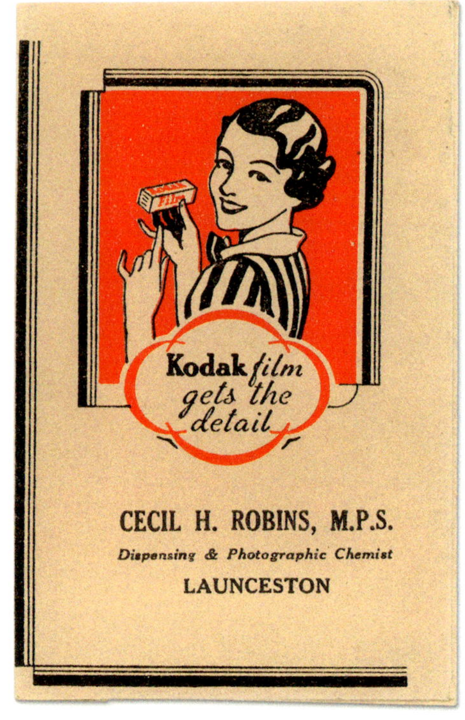
Film
Kodak film
gets the
detail
CECIL H. ROBINS, M.P.S.
Dispensing & Photographic Chemist
LAUNCESTON

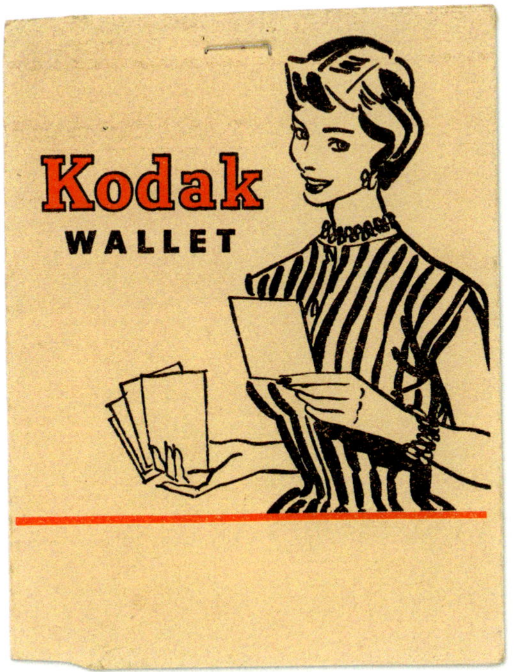

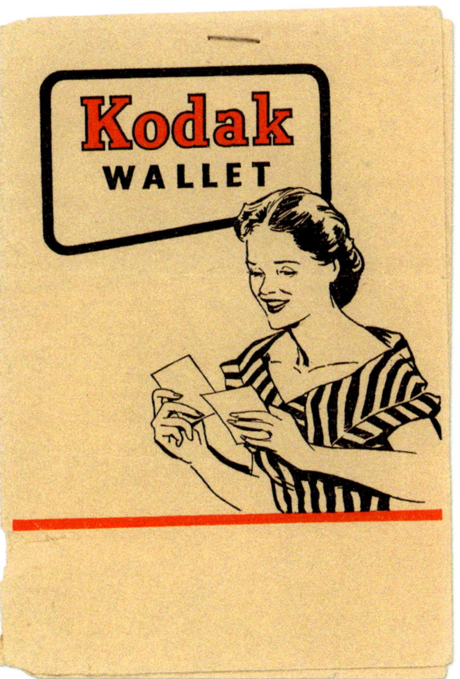

Preceding pages and next spread: Her hemlines and hairstyles changed over time, but whether her camera was a Box Brownie in the 1920s or an Instamatic in the 1960s, the smiling Kodak Girl was an aspirational model in line drawings and photographs for over fifty years.

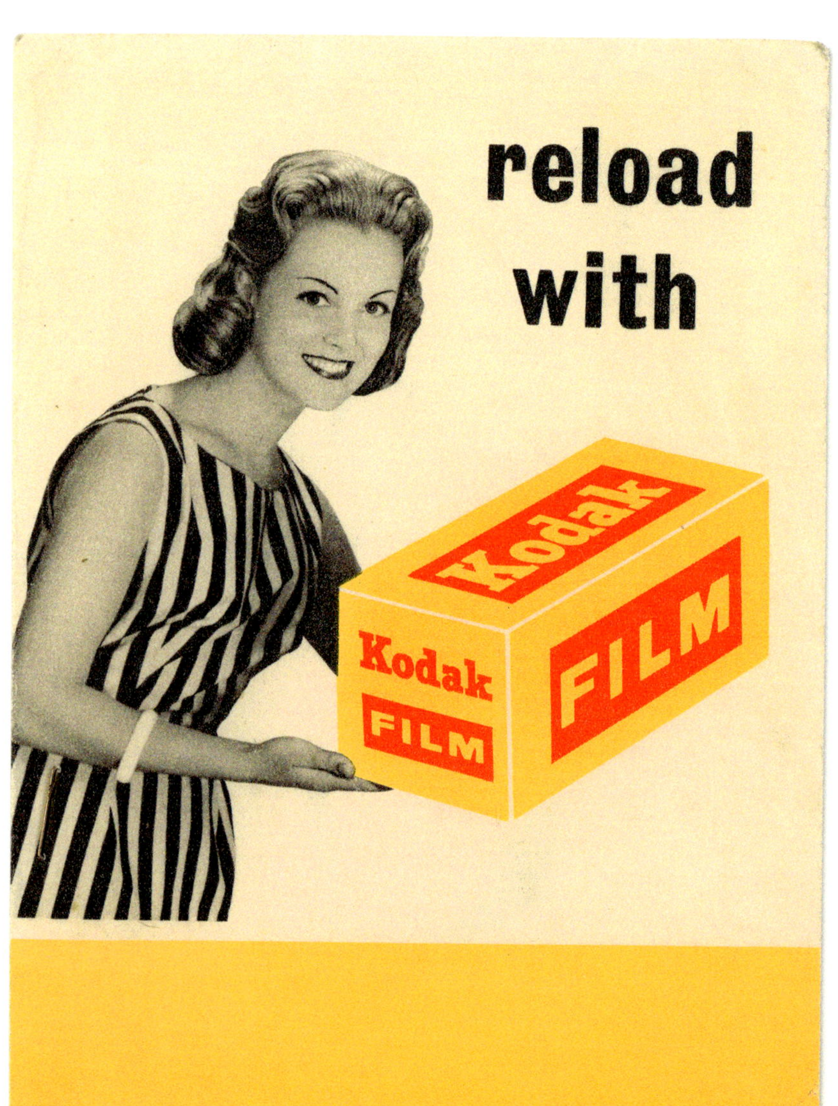

reload with
Kodak
FILM
Kodak
FILM

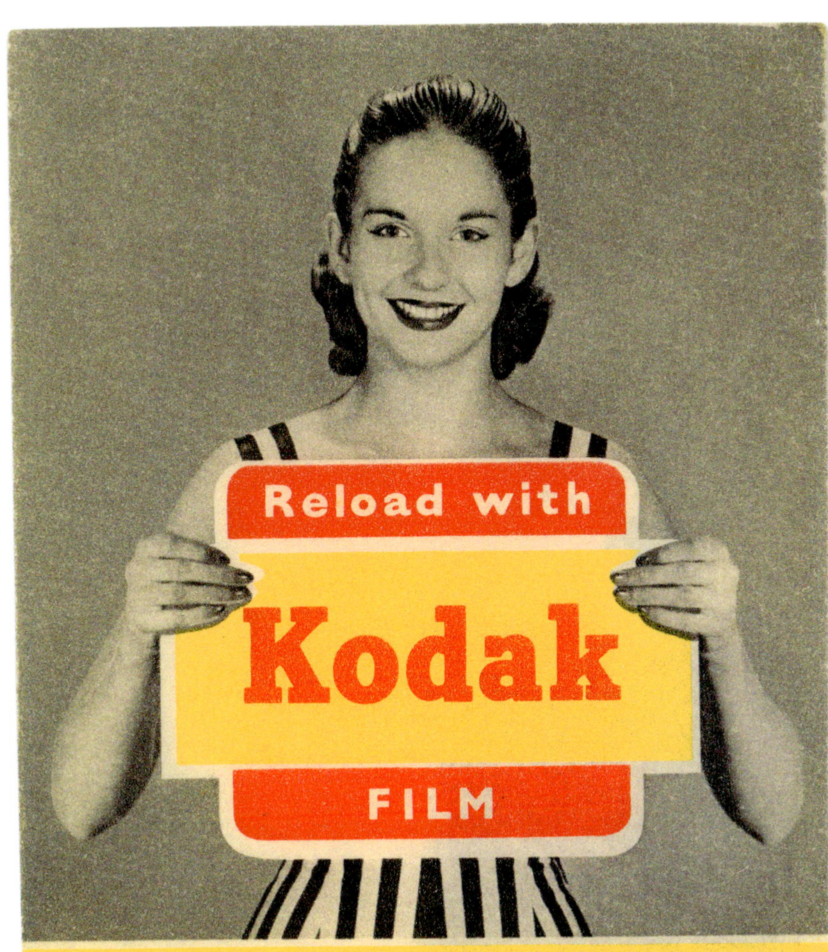
Reload with
Kodak
FILM

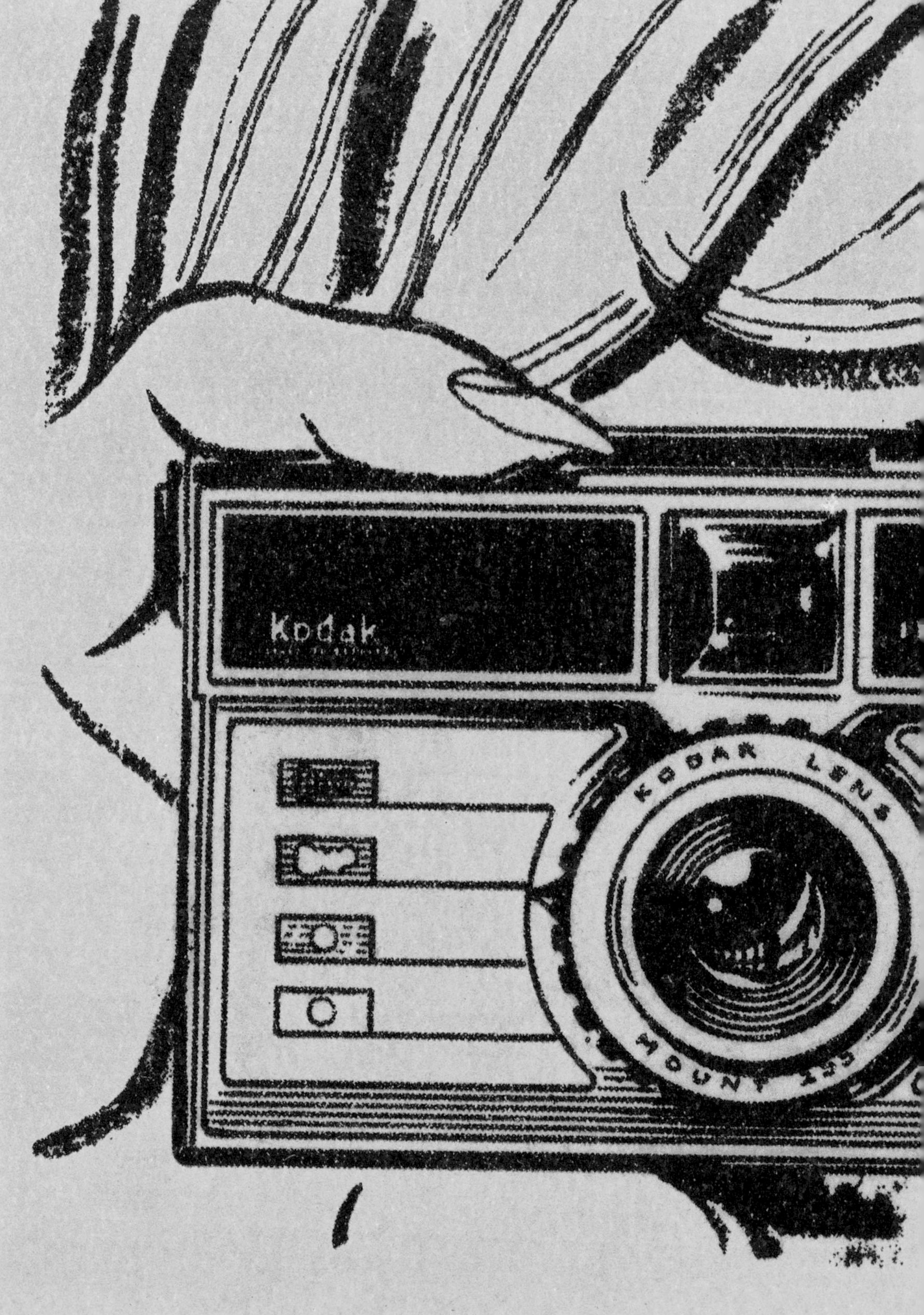
Kodak
KODAK LENS
MOUNT

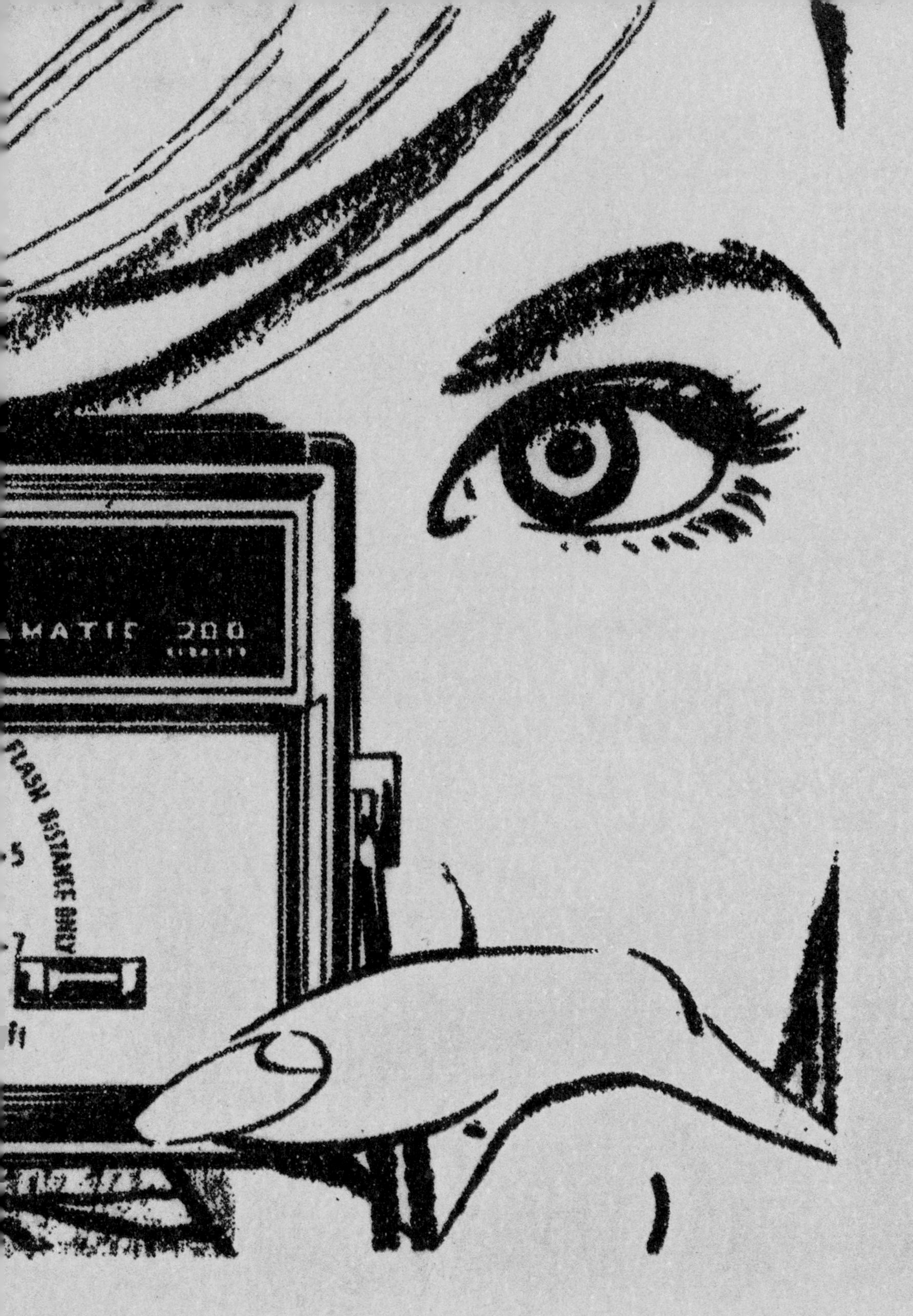
MATIC 200
FLASH DISTANCE ONLY

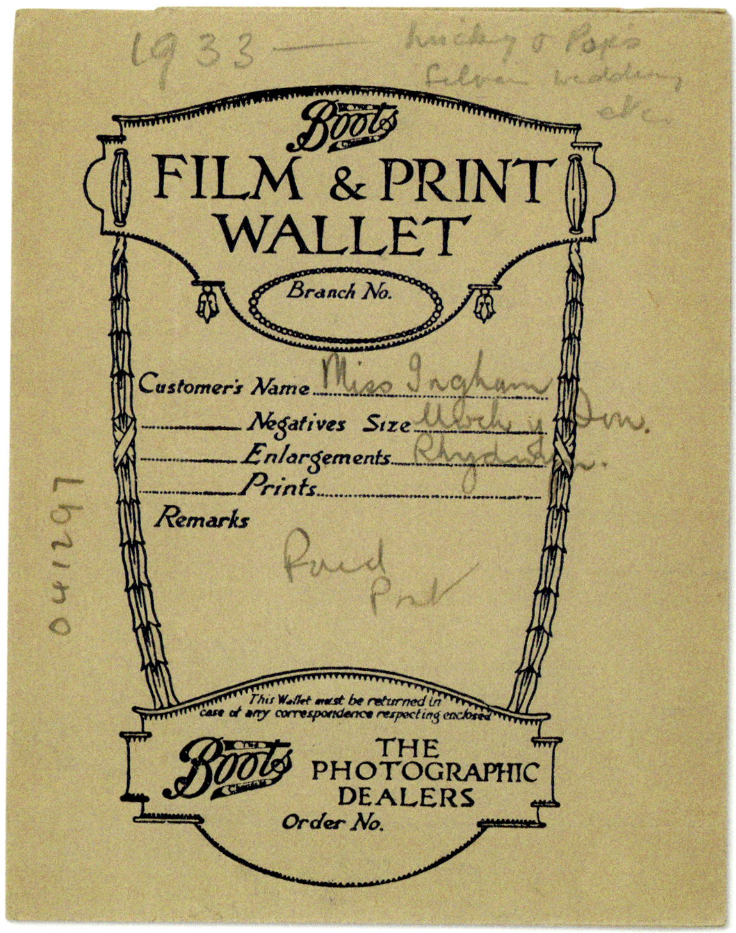

Above and following spreads: Boots the Chemist described themselves
from the early twentieth century as 'The Photographer's Chemist'. As a leading
British provider of high street developing and printing, they dispensed
photographic guidance as well as film services.

The Photographers' Chemist

While Kodak was the global leader in photographic products and supplies, the company most associated with developing and printing in Britain was Boots the Chemist. Boots began as a single herbalist shop in Nottingham in 1849 but began expanding significantly in the same years that chemists entered the photo-processing market. In 1890 Boots had ten shops, by 1900, over 200. By 1939, Boots was one of only five British companies with more than 1,000 branches, and by the 1970s they boasted over 1,600. They promoted processing prominently from the First World War, promising 'prompt and perfect service from picture to print'. By the early 1930s they noted in internal bulletins that their photographic department was 'rising like a rocket' with 800% growth: 'Far more people are using cameras – and more and more of them are coming to regard Boots as the logical place for supplies and Developing and Printing work'. Merchandising was central to this business. 'When a Photo Wallet goes over the counter', they advised staff, 'it carries more than negatives and prints.' It was as important as a prescription envelope in building a quality reputation. By 1955, Boots calculated that they were the largest photographic retailer in Britain, and their position as the number one provider for developing and printing would remain secure for the next three decades.[6]

Boots' early print wallets were very similar to the dispensing envelopes they used to supply medication. Each contained similar textual information, but the photo wallet added a few more decorative flourishes. The correspondence between the two was symbolic as well as stylistic. By making a link between dispensing and developing, and between patient and photographer, Boots could build professional conduct, even bedside manner, into their photographic offer. As they stated, in 1924, 'Boots the Chemists are willing at all times to give advice to amateurs in difficulty.' Women addressed customers in Boots' advertising, and they were also depicted as camera users, because Boots understood that the photographic market was stratified by gender. Aspirational amateur photographers, as consumers of specialist cameras and services, tended to be male; women were perceived to be less interested in technology and technique and were more likely to photograph their family. Those in the former group might spend more on gear, but there were fewer of them. Boots served, instead, what they called the 'Happy Snapper'. In 1955, Boots stated, 'We prefer the big selling and profitable part of the business.' If every customer who used a single roll of film per year, on their holiday, could be convinced to buy just one more, income could boom. Their recommendations were prescriptive, reinforcing photographic expectations and expanding sales.

Boots' illustrated envelopes, from the 1930s, firstly featured line drawings, then fuzzy half-tone prints and, later, sharper photographic images in black and white. These shifted, around 1960, to full colour. They showed happy scenes of families and pets and country and coastal locations. Boots took their photographic packaging seriously and won awards from Britain's Council of Industrial Design in the 1960s. In 1971, they commissioned a 'Photographic Design Plan' by McCann Design Associates, who undertook what they described as scientific research into subconscious desires, testing a national sample of women and men, covering a range of photographic habits. The research led to a 'disciplined house identity' that was believed to communicate superlative dependability, efficiency, modernity and value. The review changed Boots' lettering from drop-shadow upper case to an informal, slim-line, white typewriter-style face. The former blue, green, black and white scheme of 1960s packaging was changed to fresh apple green with flashes of violet and magenta. Tellingly, however, the images that dominated the wallets remained: infants and kittens, boats in the harbour and swans on the lake, all taken in bright sunlight. Tastes for fonts and colour palettes change faster than photographic fashions.

Opposite: Dynamic enlargements offered by Boots, c.1930s.

LET US ENLARGE
YOUR
FAVOURITE
SNAPS
Boots
FOR EVERYTHING PHOTOGRAPHIC

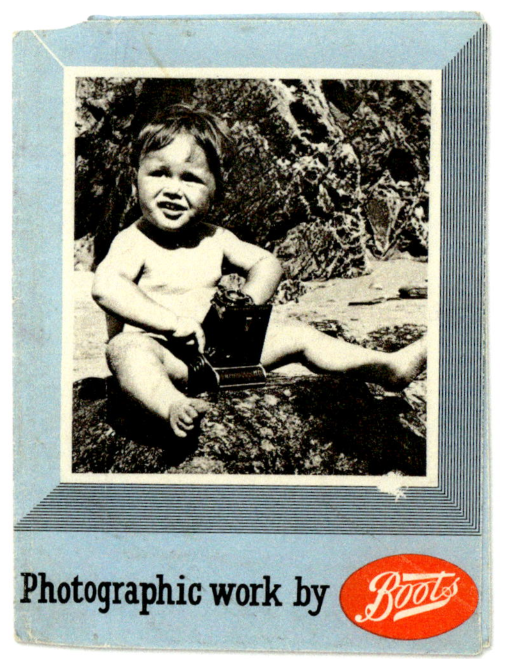

Photographic work by **Boots**

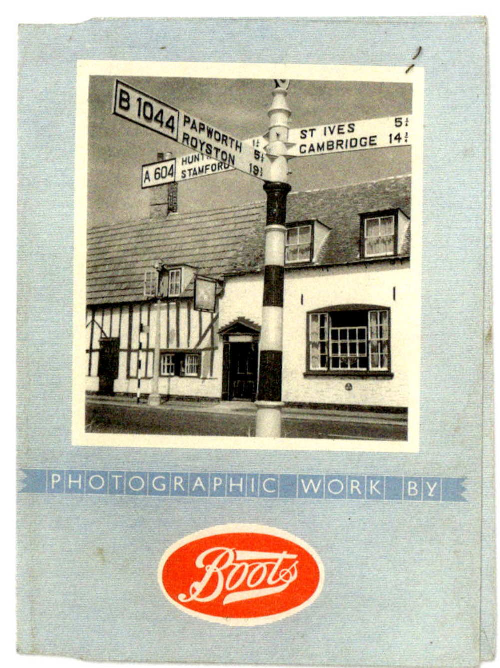

PHOTOGRAPHIC WORK BY

Boots

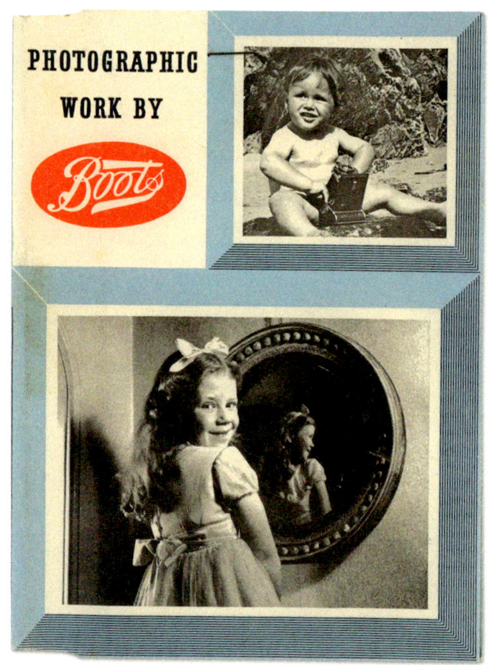

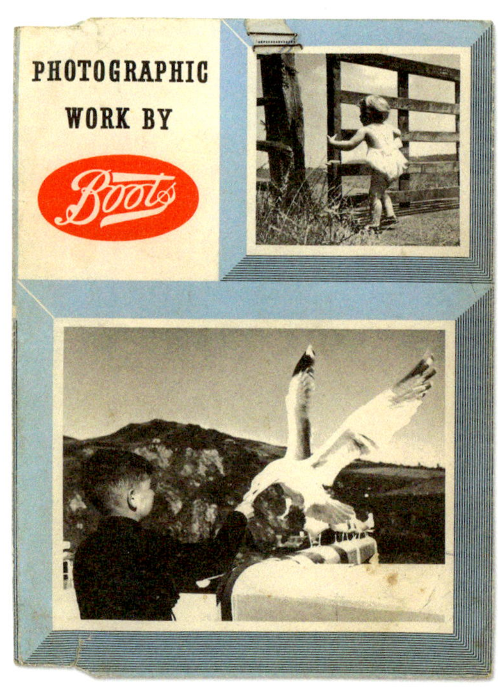

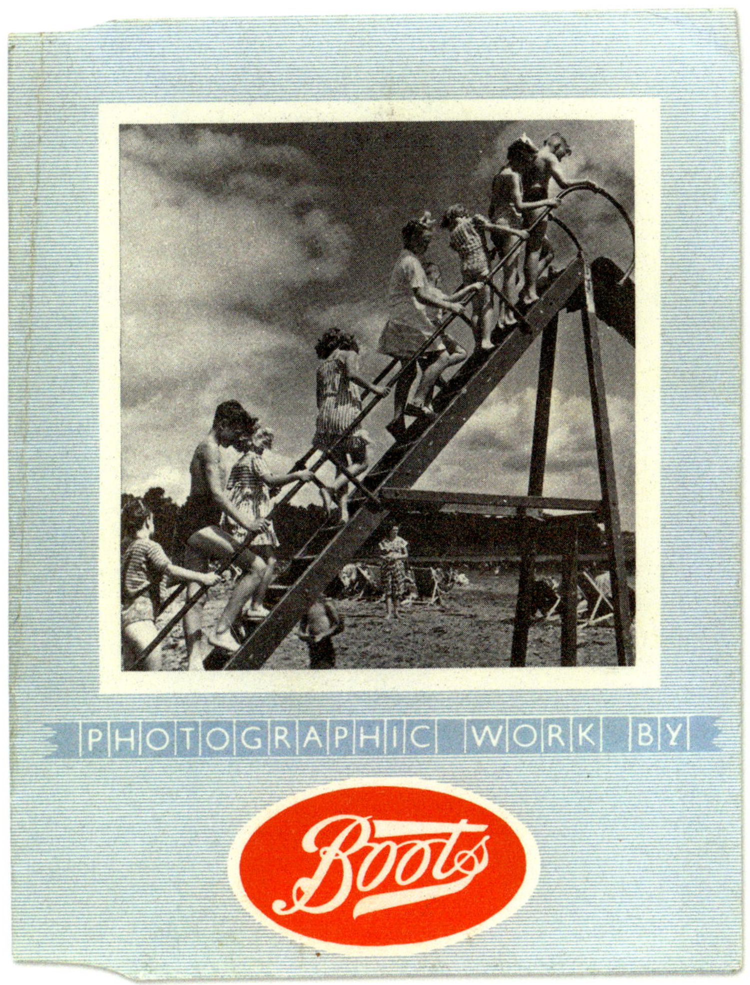

Holidays, families and playtimes on Boots wallets of the early 1950s.

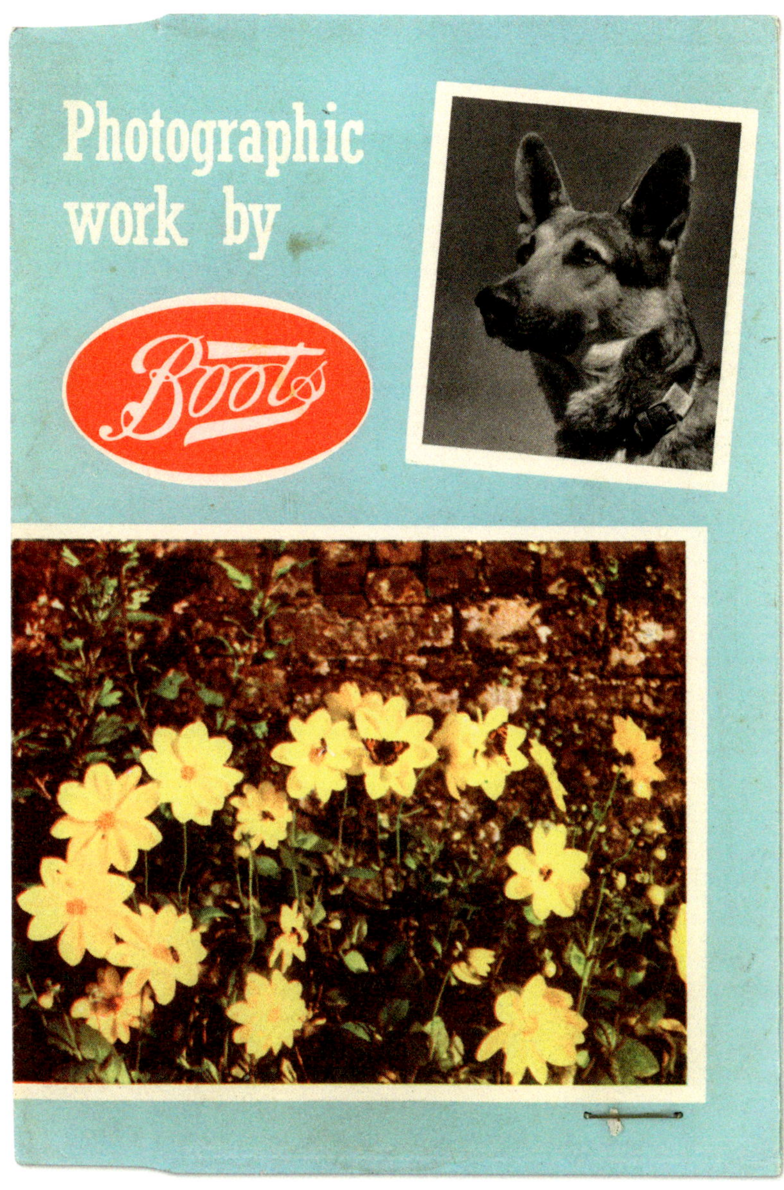

By the 1960s, colour prints and indoor flash photography
were the main promotional themes on Boots' print wallets.

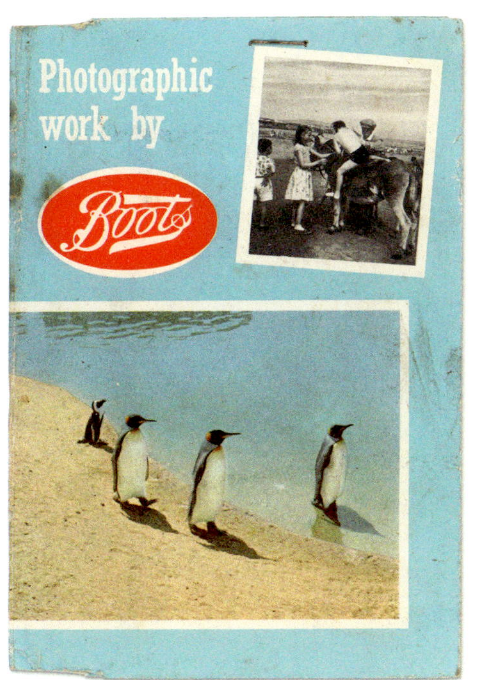

Photographic
work by
Boots

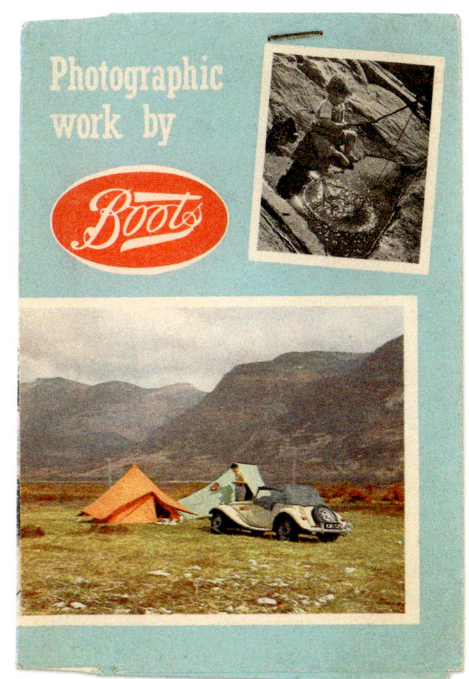

Photographic
work by
Boots

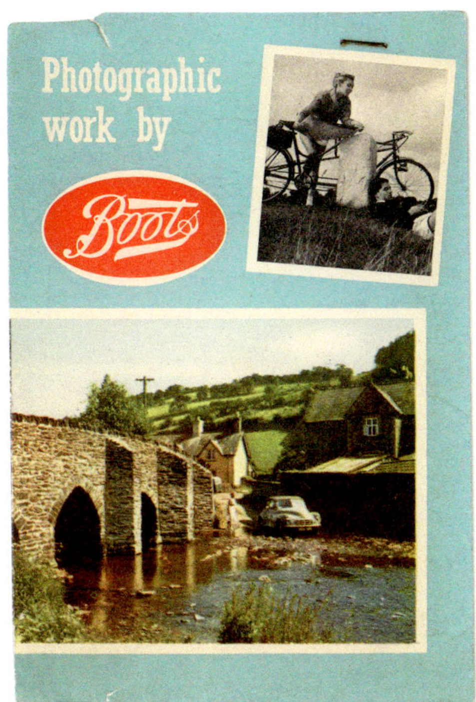

Photographic
work by
Boots

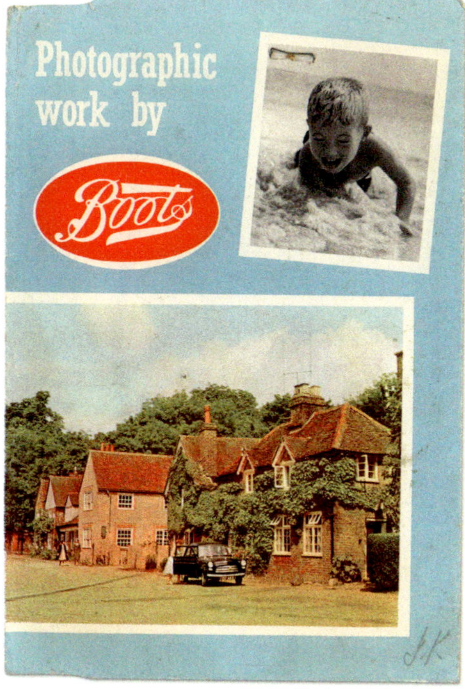

Photographic
work by
Boots

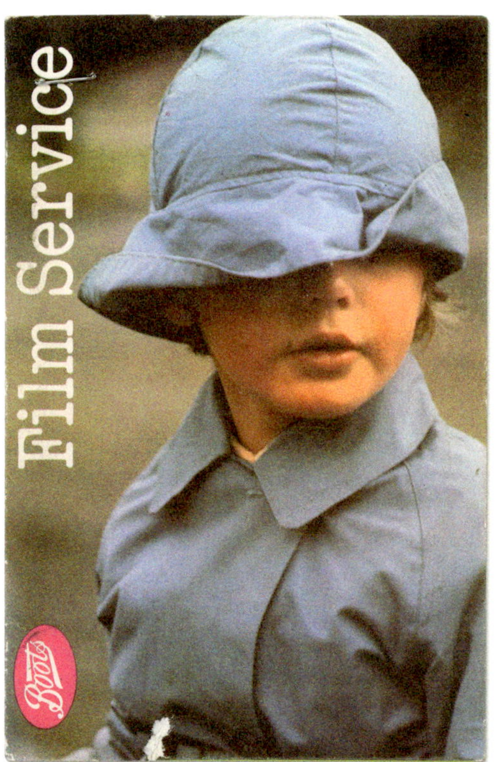

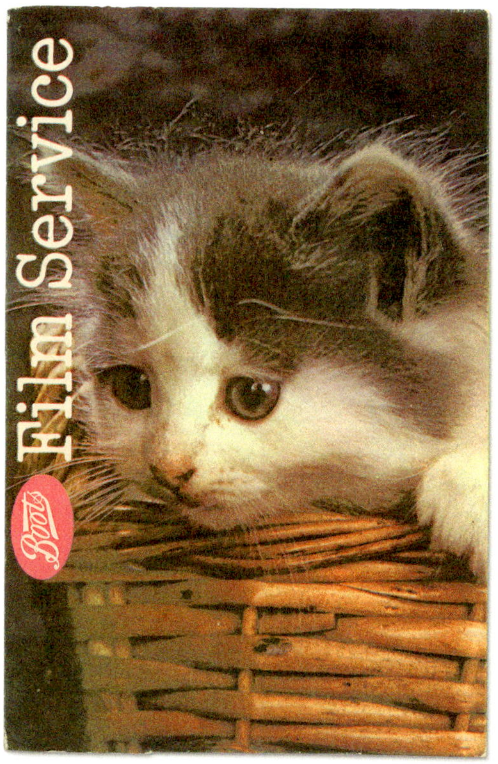

At the start of the 1970s, Boots refreshed their photographic
wallets with new typefaces and colour schemes, but
enduring subject matter – families, animals, leisure – remained.

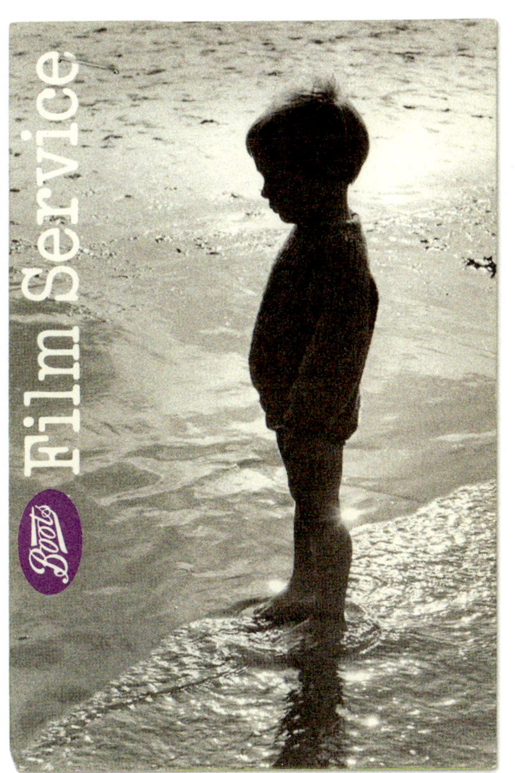
Film Service
Boots

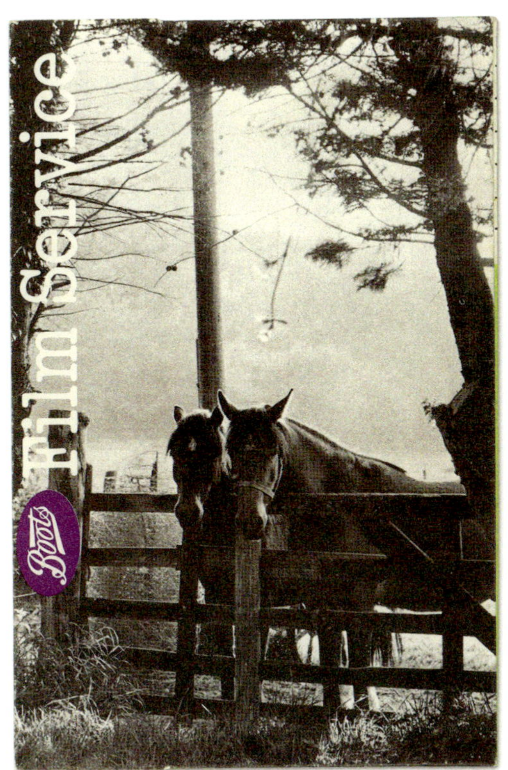
Film Service
Boots

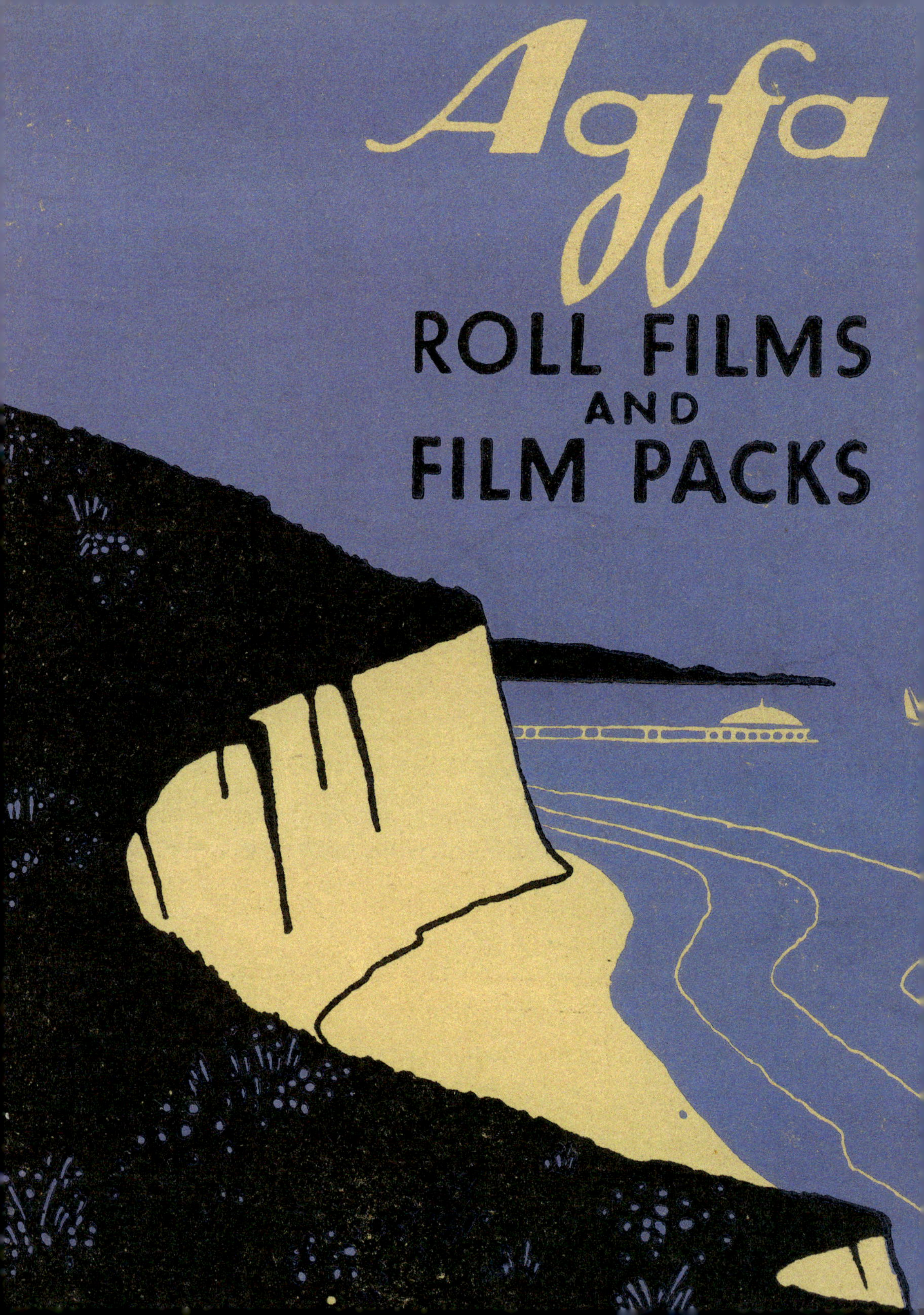
Agfa
ROLL FILMS
AND
FILM PACKS

British Film for British People?

While Kodak and Boots were the dominant providers of developing and printing in twentieth-century Britain, there were other major players and many smaller names whose businesses are now defunct and forgotten. Ilford, whose print wallets described them in the 1960s as 'today's leader in photography', were significant producers of cameras and especially film, including under the Selo brand from the 1930s. Selo film came in a red tube inside a distinctive black box with a yellow diamond at its centre. It was advertised on punchy print wallets with striped edges as eye-catching as hazard signs. Unlike American-origin Kodak, who had also developed a red, yellow and black colourway, Selo was patriotically marketed as 'British made to suit British climate'. Its brand mascot was a soldier in red or yellow trousers, a black jacket with the diamond motif and a sentry's cap. Advertising material stated, 'The Selo Soldier Salutes you!' At carnivals in the 1930s, Ilford employees would dress in Selo soldier uniforms to wave Union Jacks on parade floats. On photo wallets, the soldier bows with gratitude for the purchase, stands guard next to the print and flies the flag for Selo services. Selo film promised novices that good photographs were possible 'from six in the morning until seven in the evening' in the summer, and 'in mid-winter from ten in the morning until two in the afternoon'. Photography with a cheap camera had a narrow timeframe for success in this period, which Ilford aimed to extend: 'There was a time when photography was an occupation for the sunny hours. Whenever the sun went behind a cloud, the camera went back in its case.' By the 1930s, they claimed, with Selo film, 'anything that can be seen can be photographed'.

Ensign film was advertised with a similar national narrative at the end of the First World War as 'British Film for British People'. Its print wallets in the 1930s featured an angular flash of streaking light to show photography's speed and energy. The brand character waved an undulating red and blue Ensign banner and wore the winged helmet of Hermes. The divine messenger carried both the customers' prints and illuminating advice on successful photography. Don't do it, he said, 'when your subject is in

Opposite: The coastal location on this interwar Agfa wallet,
with white cliffs and pier, could equally suggest an English
or German beach at a time when patriotic narratives drove sales.

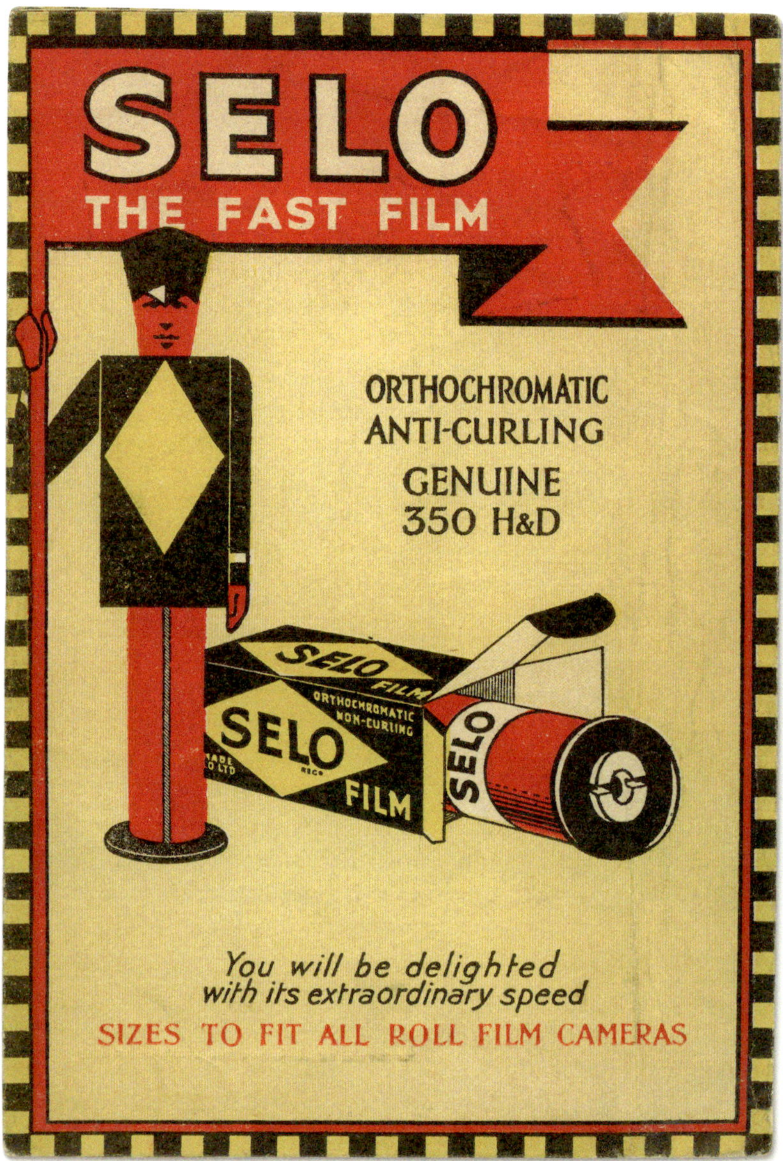

Pre-Second World War Selo, Ensign and Novex personified
film characters conveyed authority, speed and simplicity.

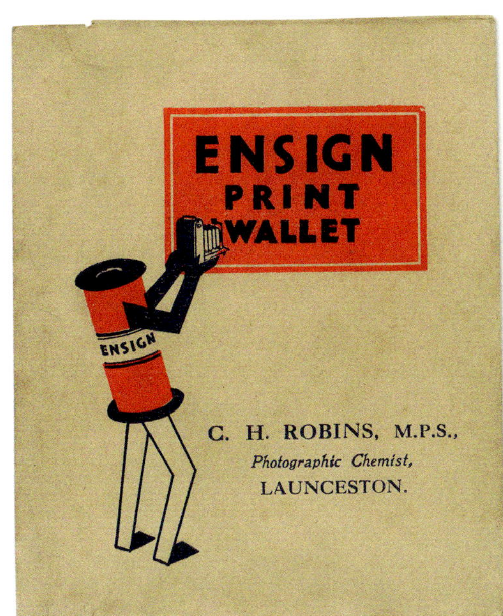

ENSIGN
PRINT
WALLET
ENSIGN
C. H. ROBINS, M.P.S.,
Photographic Chemist,
LAUNCESTON.

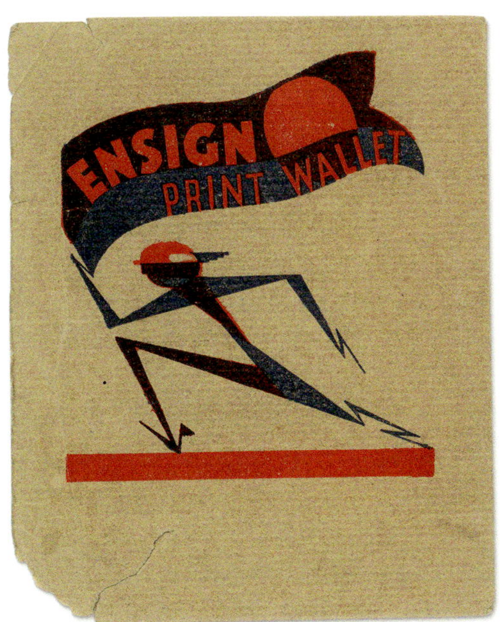

ENSIGN
PRINT WALLET

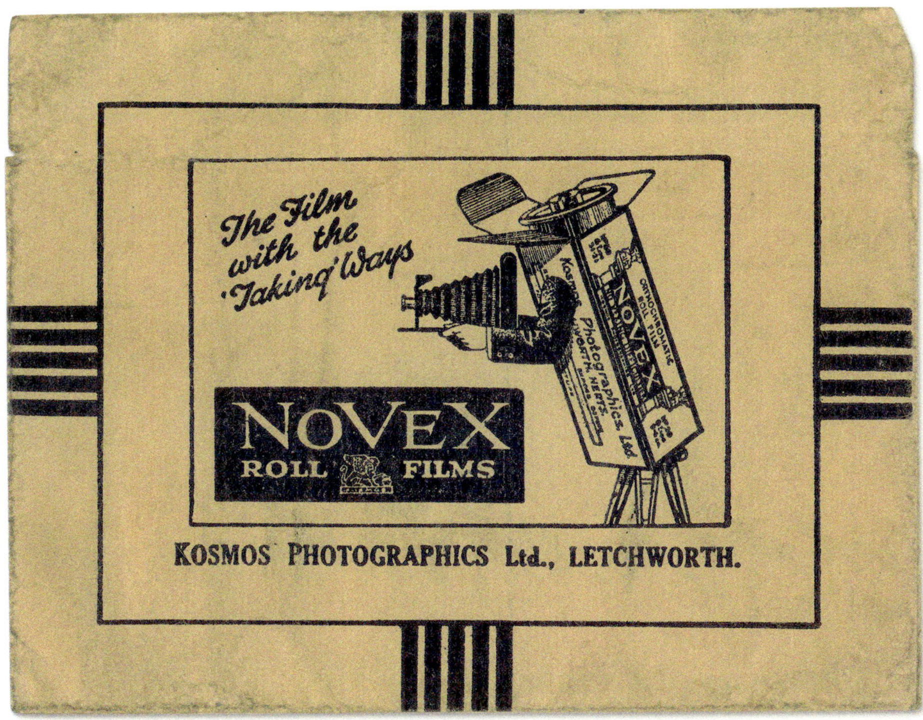

The Film
with the
'Taking' Ways
NOVEX
ROLL FILMS
ORTHOCHROMATIC
ROLL FILMS
NOVEX
Kosmos
Photographics Ltd.
LETCHWORTH, HERTS.
KOSMOS PHOTOGRAPHICS Ltd., LETCHWORTH.

deep shadows'. Alternative versions had a red roll of film giving avuncular advice, leaning on a walking cane, hands on hips, full of swagger. '90% of your pictures will probably be made of your friends', the personified film asserted confidently. 'Do not put them in front of brick walls, as though they were going to be shot.' The character illustrated both the contents of the camera and its operator in the print wallet depictions. Ensign Film was the omniscient 'full-of-detail film that sees everything' but its red mascot, with folding film arms and legs, was oddly eyeless.

The Britishness that many print wallets trumpeted was due not only to Kodak's dominance as an American-born business, but also to rival quality products imported from Germany. Wallets in the 1930s advertised Agfa Isochrom film in red, blue and yellow packaging; the yellow band on the red roll of film circled the world. Agfa also advertised their German products on wallets that suggested English seaside locations with white cliffs and a pier under blue skies. British beaches and rural sites feature prominently as imagined holiday destinations at a time when international travel was a rare luxury for most. Significant sites in London, from Buckingham Palace to Big Ben, also appeared on print wallets, but attention was distributed across all four nations as processors stretched from Aberdeen to Belfast. Some depictions are localised. The half-timbered buildings and cobbled streets that serve as wallet illustrations showed the historic sites where processors were based, from Gloucester to Edinburgh, but also photography's appropriate subjects. Processors boasted of their up-to-date technology and modern production methods, but their image models aligned with Pictorialist taste and ideals of British heritage, which emphasised the rural and the ancient.

Britishness on print wallets was clearly perceived to be universally white; every illustrated photographer and subject is such. This racialised assumption is made visible in mid-century illustrations showing silhouetted child-like black figures with spiky hair, hooped earrings, bare feet and grass skirts under palm trees trying to fathom photographic technology at a time when print wallets proudly traded under imperialist brand names. Both Timothy Whites & Taylors, and Thompson & Capper Ltd, were dispensing chemists with photographic specialisms and multiple branches across the country; both had pre-photographic origins in pharmacy. Both adapted the same racist cartoon on their wallets. Its figures are depicted as innocents to whom photography is mystifying; the viewer and consumer is clearly meant to feel culturally superior in their

Opposite: Imperialist superiority infused British photo wallets visually and verbally.
J. B. Wilson photographic chemists, c.1920s.

sophisticated knowledge of camera handling. Photographic guidance on 'colour sensitivity' also reproduced assumptions about light skin. Selo film, for example, was sold in the 1930s on its ability to render colour tones in monochrome where other films were not so accurate; 'a sun-burnt girl wearing a blue dress would photograph almost like a negress in a white frock' was the example provided. A Kodak wallet of the 1960s, when colour photography was promoted, shows a blonde, white child holding a black-faced golliwog. Colour values are more than technical; they perpetuate power relations.

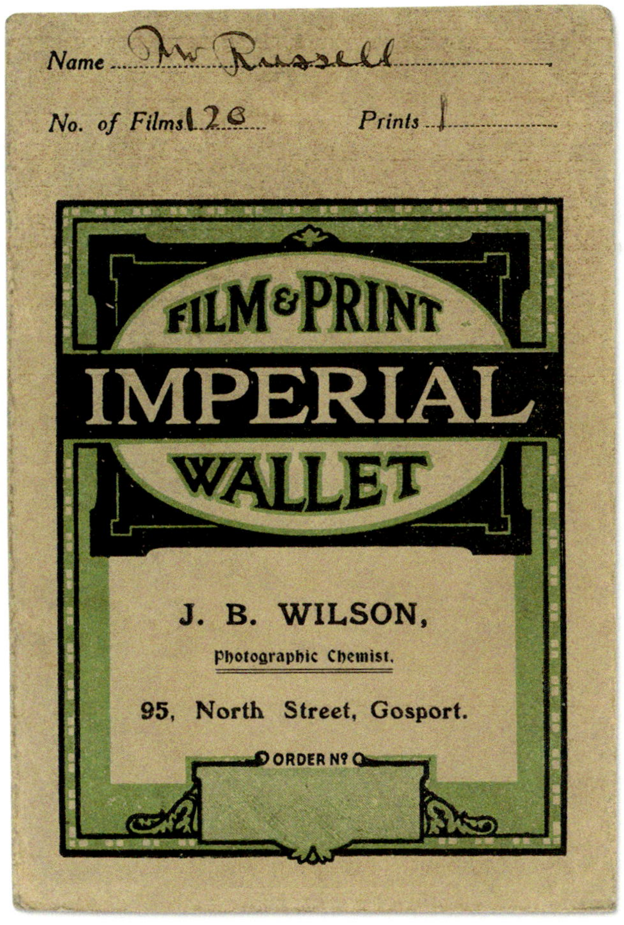

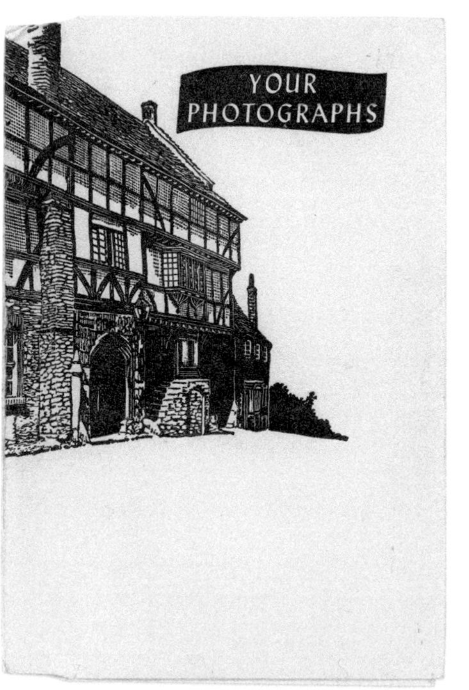
YOUR PHOTOGRAPHS

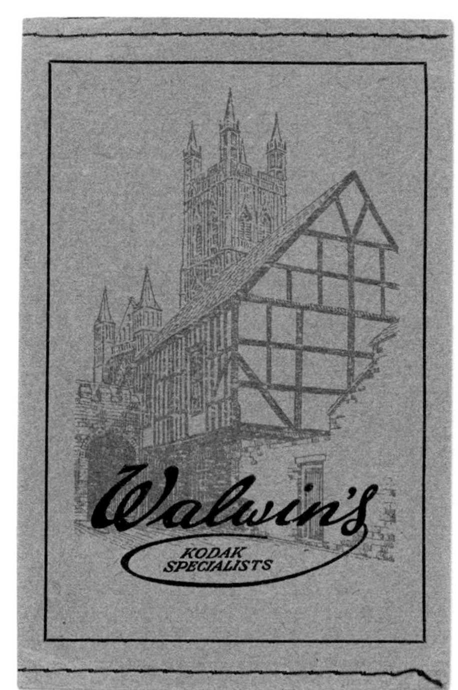
Walwin's
KODAK SPECIALISTS

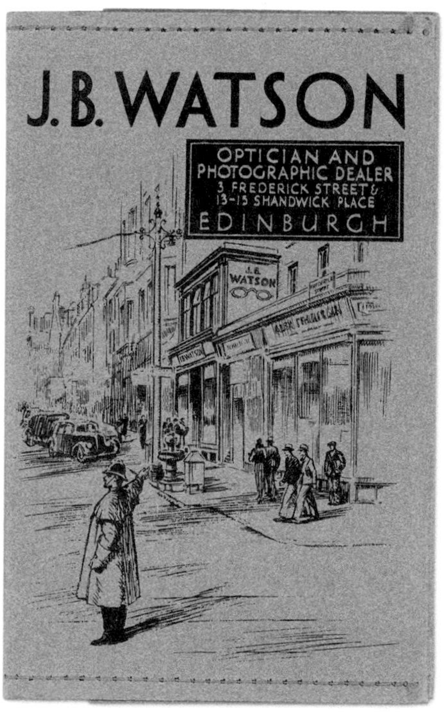
J.B.WATSON
OPTICIAN AND PHOTOGRAPHIC DEALER
3 FREDERICK STREET &
13-15 SHANDWICK PLACE
EDINBURGH
J.B. WATSON

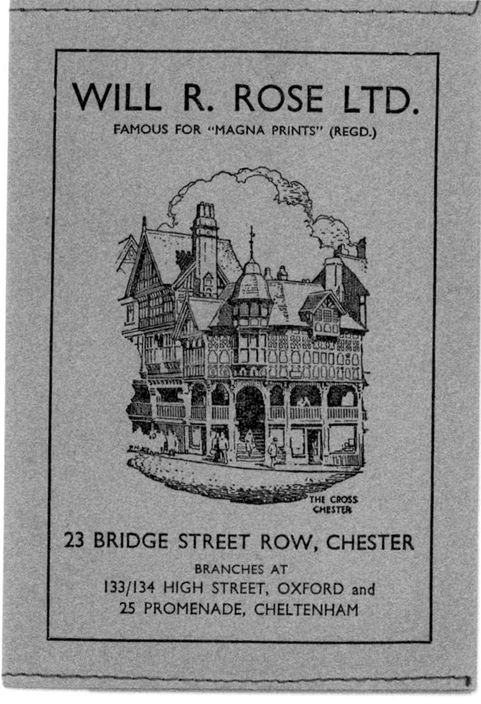
WILL R. ROSE LTD.
FAMOUS FOR "MAGNA PRINTS" (REGD.)
THE CROSS CHESTER
23 BRIDGE STREET ROW, CHESTER
BRANCHES AT
133/134 HIGH STREET, OXFORD and
25 PROMENADE, CHELTENHAM

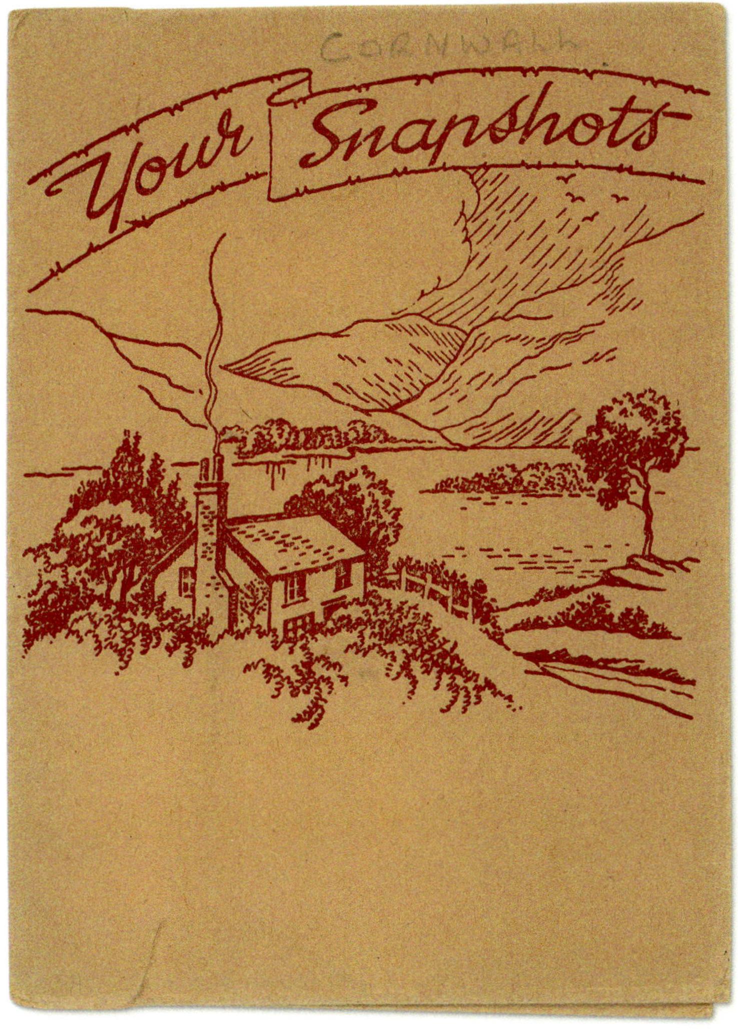

Above and opposite: Rural cottage and castles, along with historic cityscapes, demonstrated British national heritage. Wallets, from the 1920s to the 1950s, depicted suitable subjects and processors' locations.

Next spread: The association of popular photography with holidaymaking is demonstrated by wallets from the 1920s through to the 1950s featuring blue skies, sailing boats and seagulls.

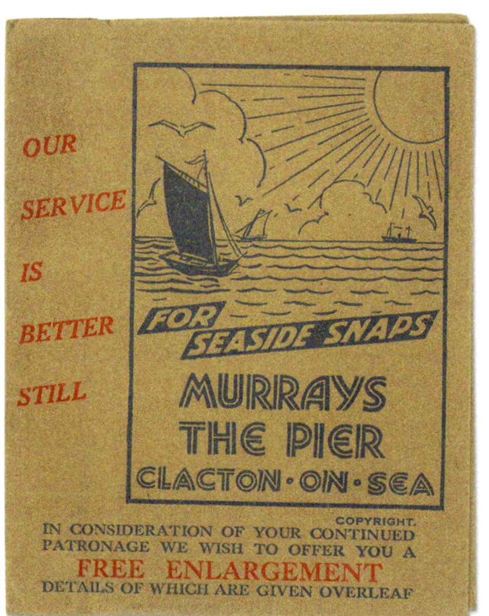
OUR
SERVICE
IS
BETTER
STILL
FOR SEASIDE SNAPS
MURRAYS
THE PIER
CLACTON·ON·SEA
COPYRIGHT.
IN CONSIDERATION OF YOUR CONTINUED
PATRONAGE WE WISH TO OFFER YOU A
FREE ENLARGEMENT
DETAILS OF WHICH ARE GIVEN OVERLEAF

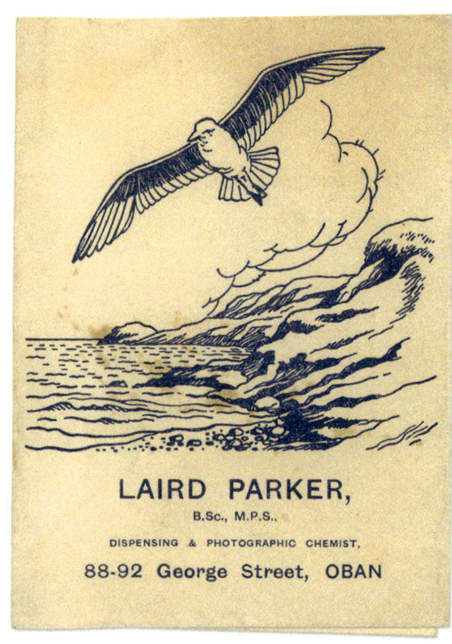
LAIRD PARKER,
B.Sc., M.P.S.,
DISPENSING & PHOTOGRAPHIC CHEMIST,
88-92 George Street, OBAN

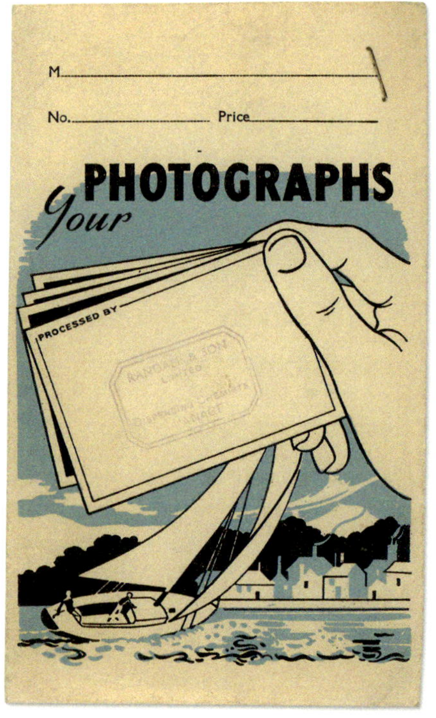
M.
No.
Price
Your PHOTOGRAPHS
PROCESSED BY

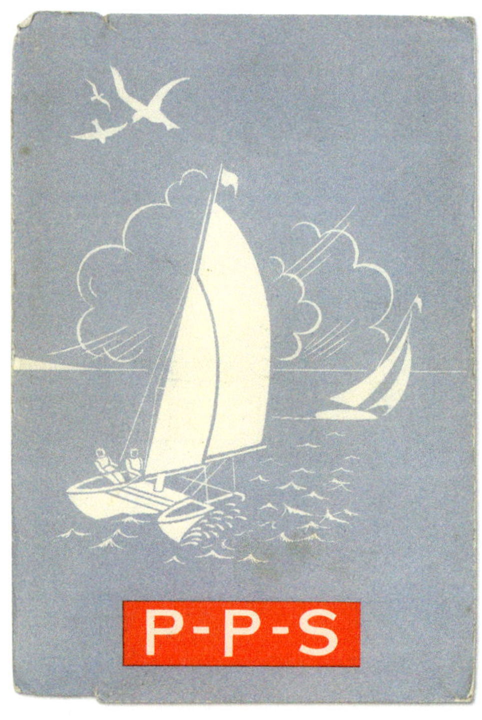
P-P-S

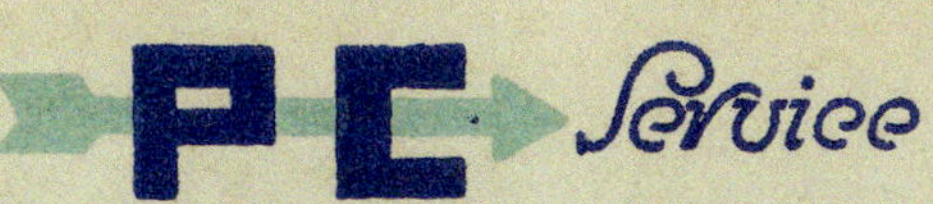

PC Service

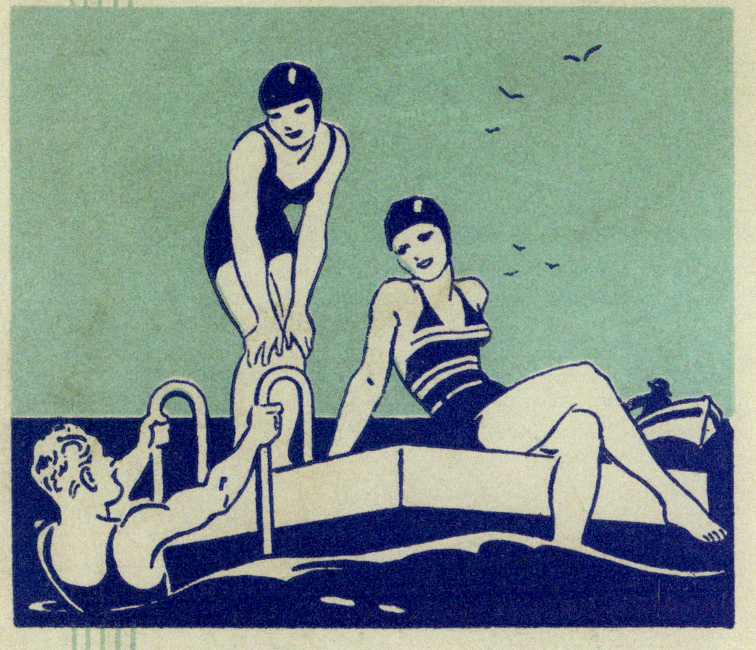

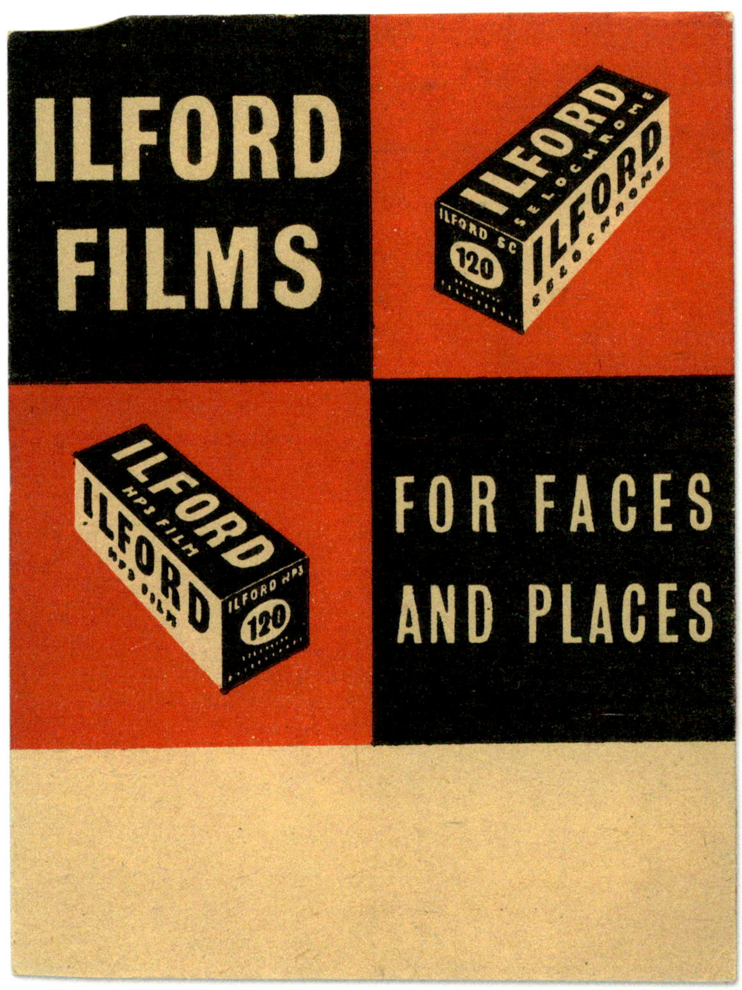

Ilford, a major British film producer, promised year-round
capabilities for capturing 'faces and places' from the 1940s.

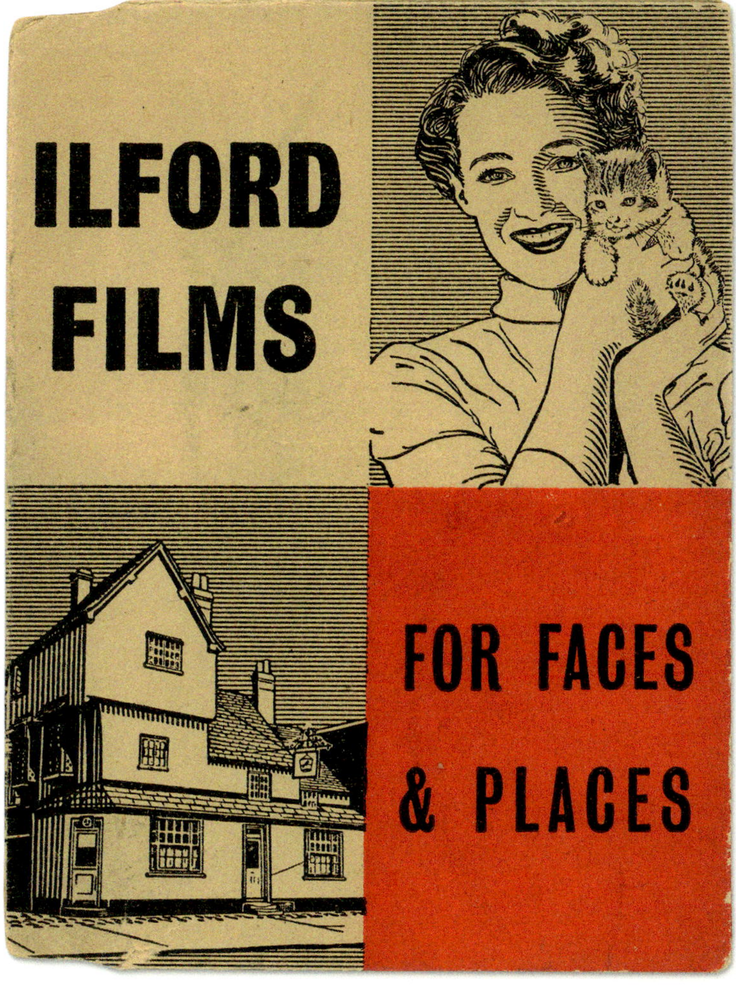
ILFORD
FILMS
FOR FACES
& PLACES

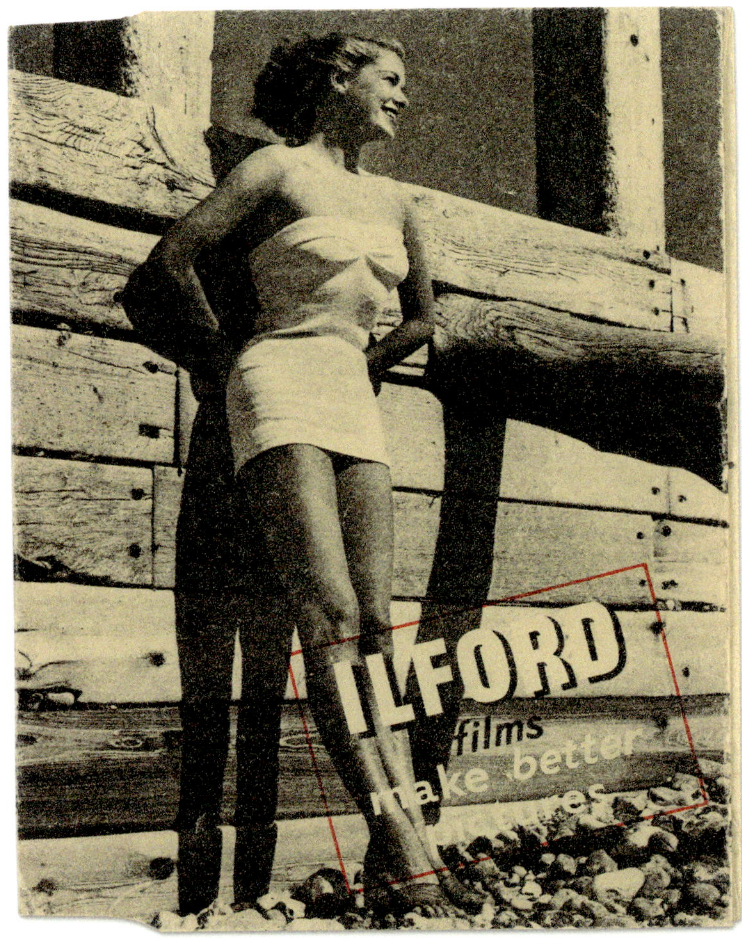

Ilford wallets equally featured cheesecake and beefcake in the 1950s and 1960s.

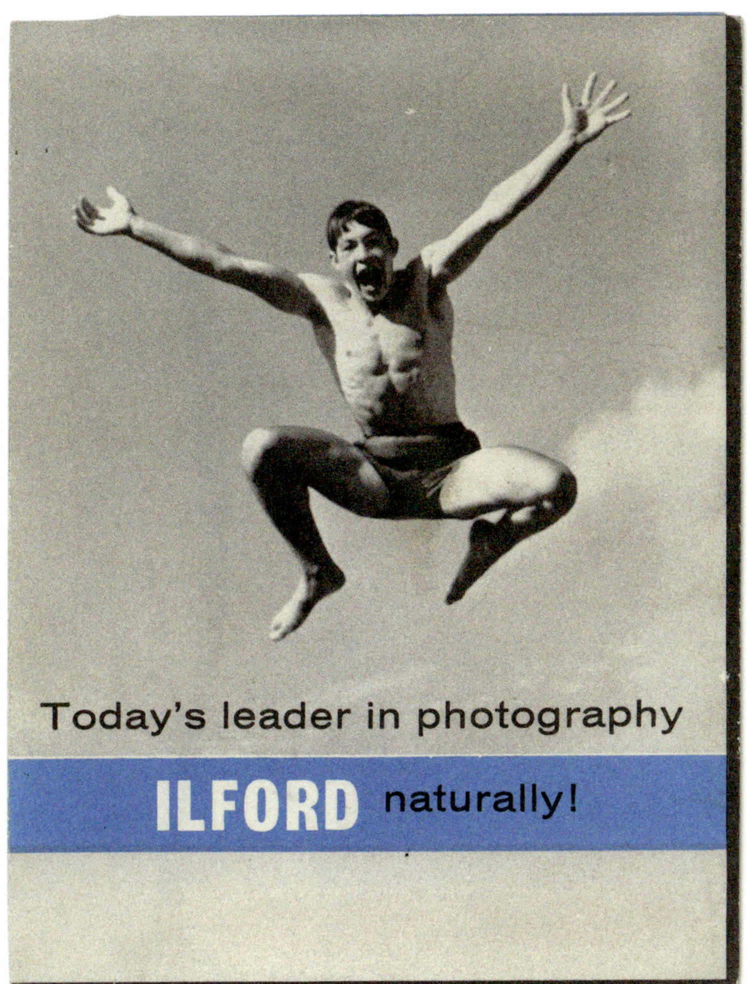

Today's leader in photography
ILFORD naturally!

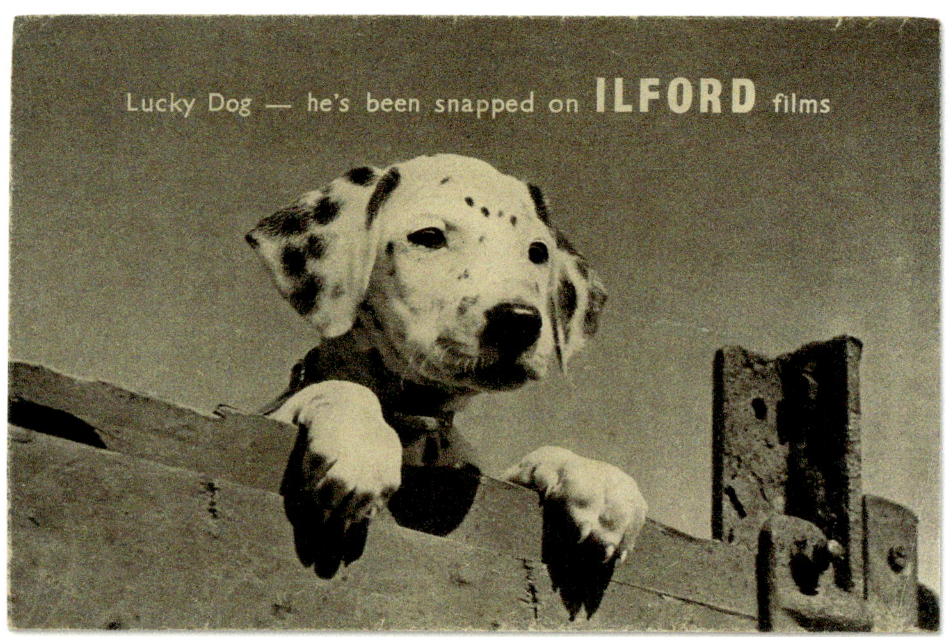

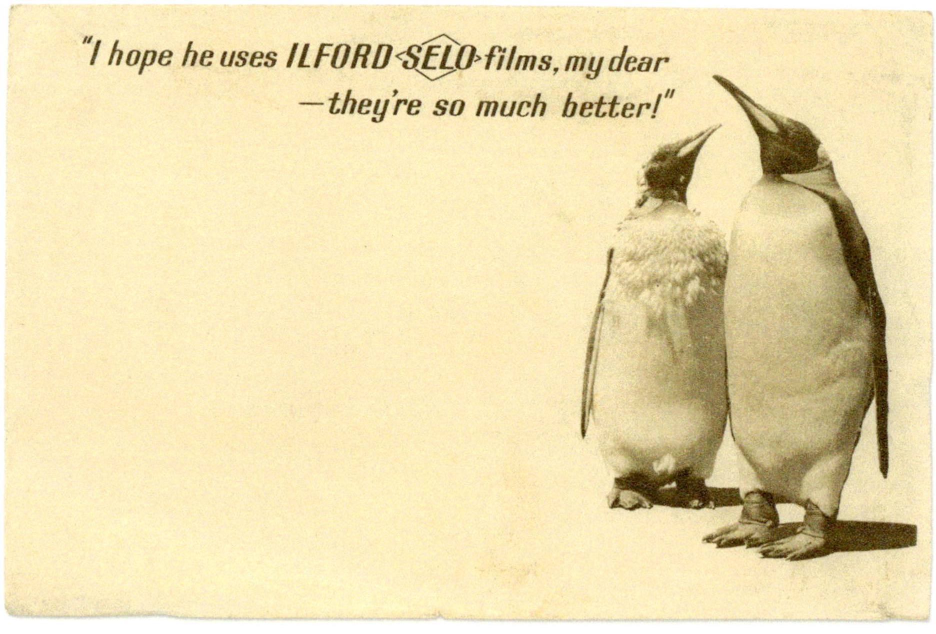

Photography at the zoo, this playful 1940s wallet suggests, has produced
aesthetic discernment in posing penguins. A Dalmatian, from the 1950s,
is similarly blessed by Ilford film.

Be snap-happy with

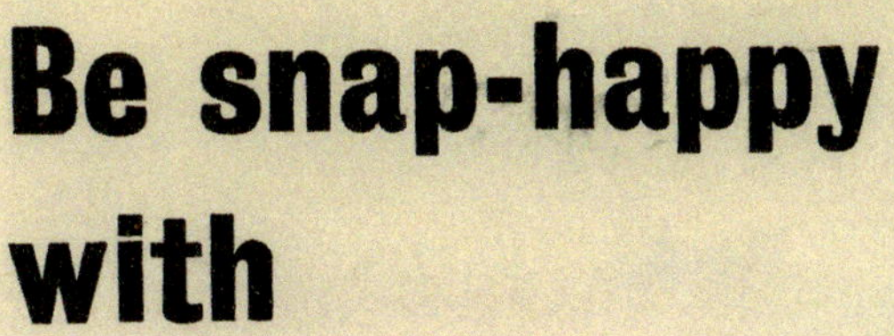

films

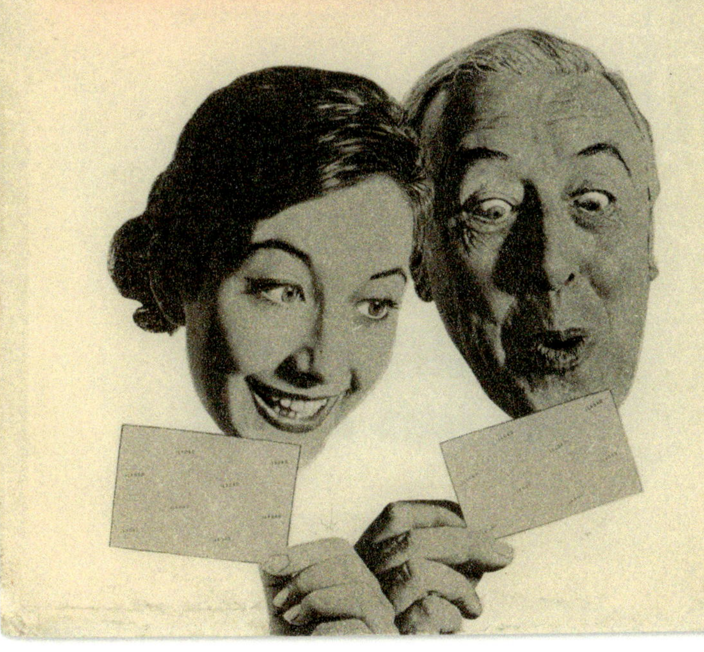

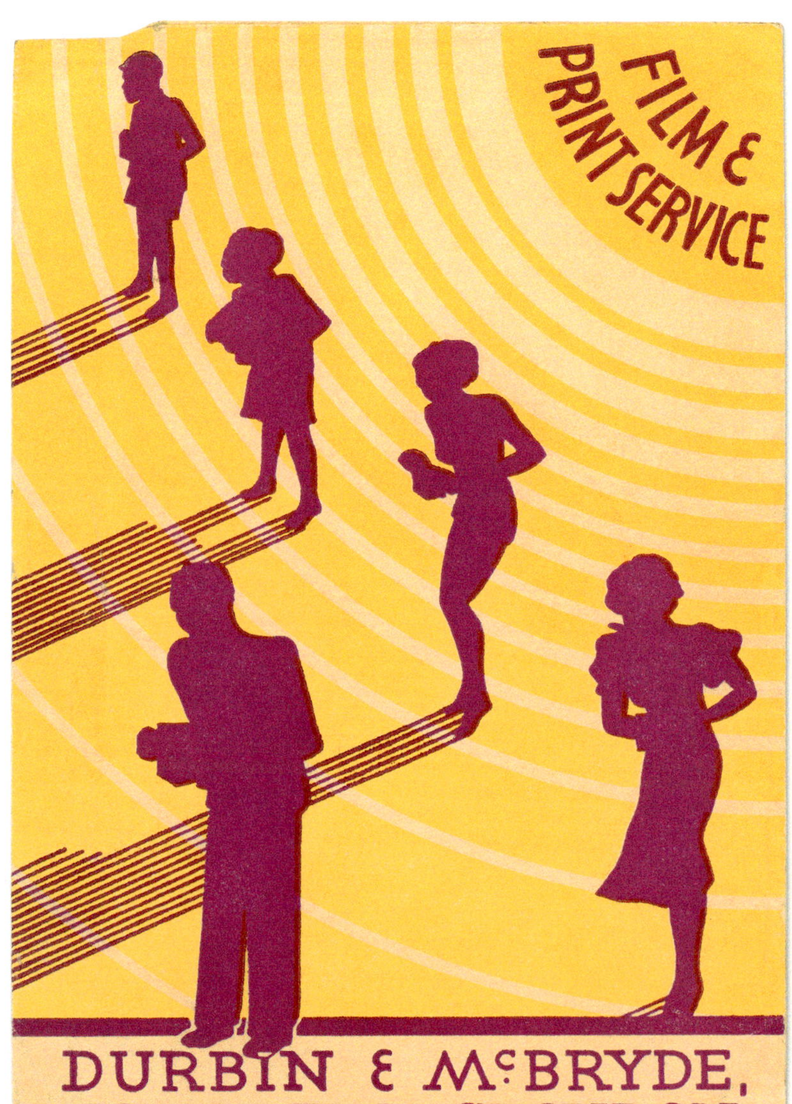

FILM &
PRINT SERVICE
DURBIN & McBRYDE,
NORTH END, CROYDON.

Dull Photographs Without Life

The visual models on print wallets suggested that sitters should smile rather than cry, subjects should be timeless rather than faddish, and the sun should always be shining. Their text explicitly told novice photographers what to do. Although photography was regularly described by all processors as easy and simple, it clearly needed to be learned and explained. Sometimes this guidance was outlined negatively. 'Do not miss your chances', unprepared photographers were warned. For good composition: 'Do not get sky in picture'. To avoid blur: 'Do not breathe'. Getting a photograph that was correctly framed, exposed and in focus was a challenge with the limited capacities of box cameras, and in the early decades of the twentieth century, there were only eight chances per roll of film to get it right. Photographers were advised 'beware of snaps when the sun is very low' and 'keep away from houses and trees' but too much light was as problematic as too much shadow. Photographers must 'wait until the sun is behind cloud at the seaside'.

For those who got it wrong, interwar processors offered 'finishing' services where a resident artist could add cloud effects, for example, into blank grey skies. Other failures were so complete that processors would not print them. Ilford marked up negatives that they felt would not make 'acceptable pictures' and isolated them in a special section of the wallet marked with a list of faults. They acknowledged, however, that photographers might still want to see the photographs, even if emotional attachment seemed less important to the company than technical merit: 'if these notched negatives are of such personal value that you would prefer to have a print regardless of the poor photographic quality', they said, 'then ask your photographic dealer to order re-prints, marking the order: PRINT REGARDLESS.'

My favourite wallet examples are those that guide without judgement and demonstrate through design. In an interwar example by Durbin & McBryde of Croydon, purple silhouette figures of boy, girl, woman and man are positioned geometrically in a graphic environment of solar rings, radiating out from the 'film & print service' written at the centre of the yellow sun. They outline photography's democratic appeal across all ages and genders, while simultaneously showing a photographic golden rule: keep your light source behind you.

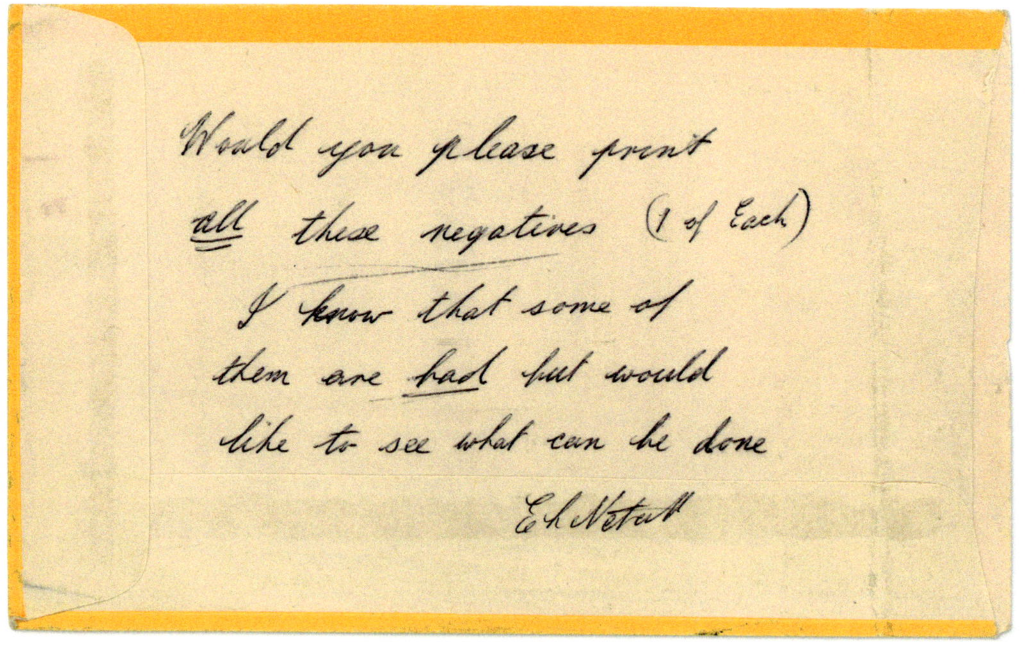

A handwritten request to a processor demonstrates that photographs' sentimental value could trump technical merit: 'Would you please print <u>all</u> these negatives (1 of each). I know that some of them are <u>bad</u> but would like to see what can be done.'

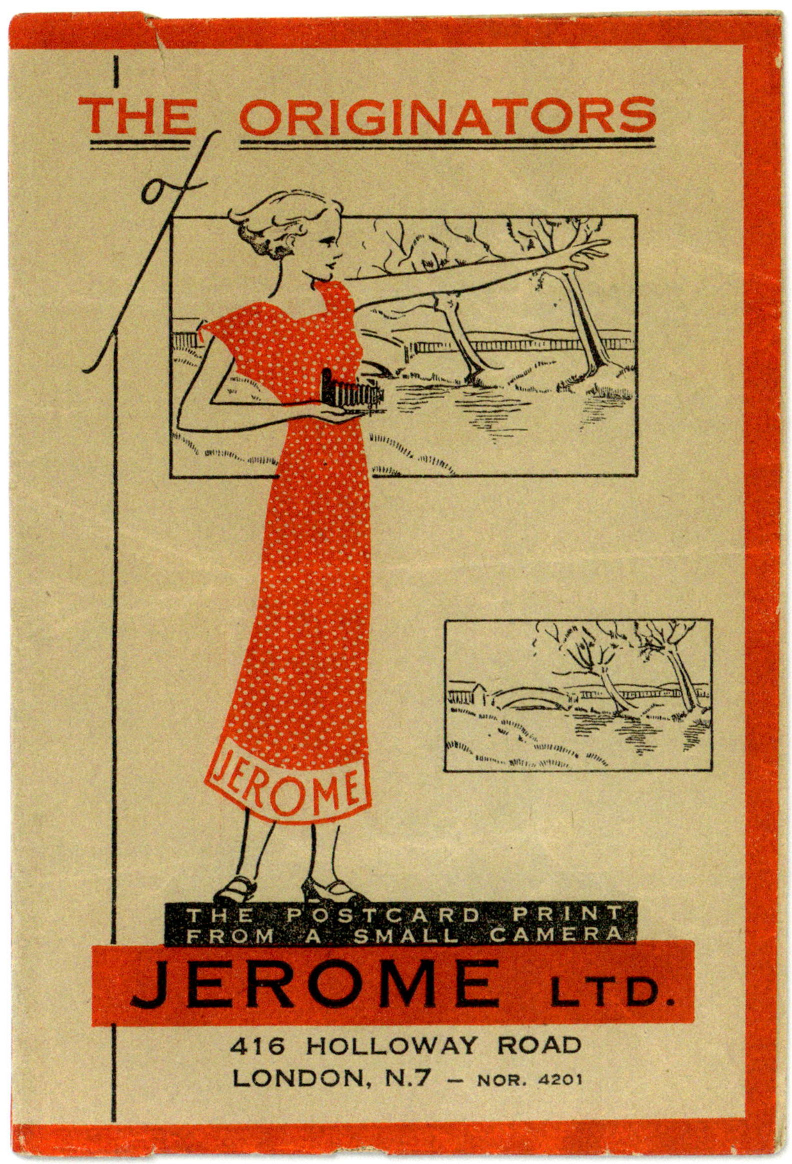

Jerome's 1930s advertising character wore a red spotted dress with the company name at the hem. With an extended arm, she draws attention to enlarging services while demonstrating how to measure photographic distance and scale.

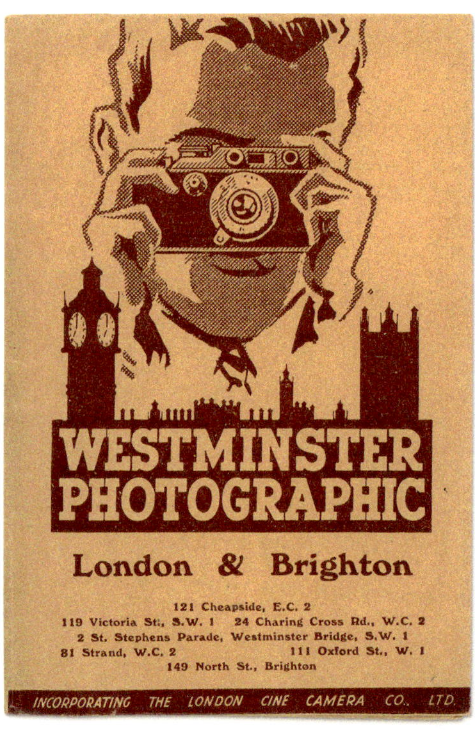

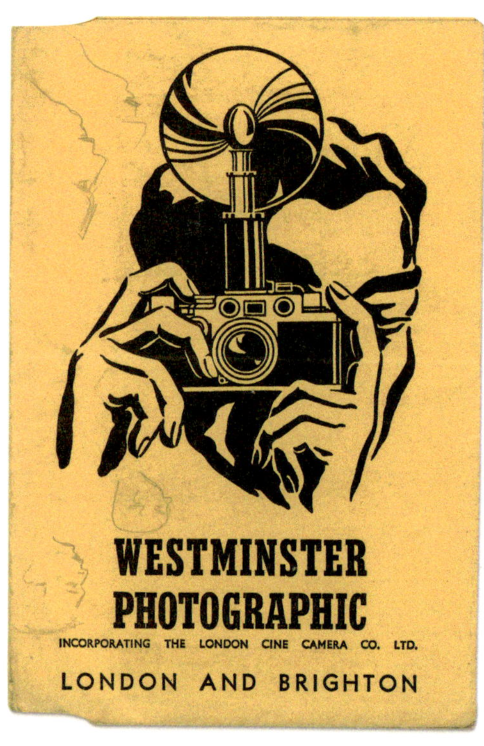

With Brylcreemed hair and an arched brow, the heroic figure
concealed behind an eye-level device at the centre of Westminster
Photographic's wallets, c.1950s, is part-man, part-camera.

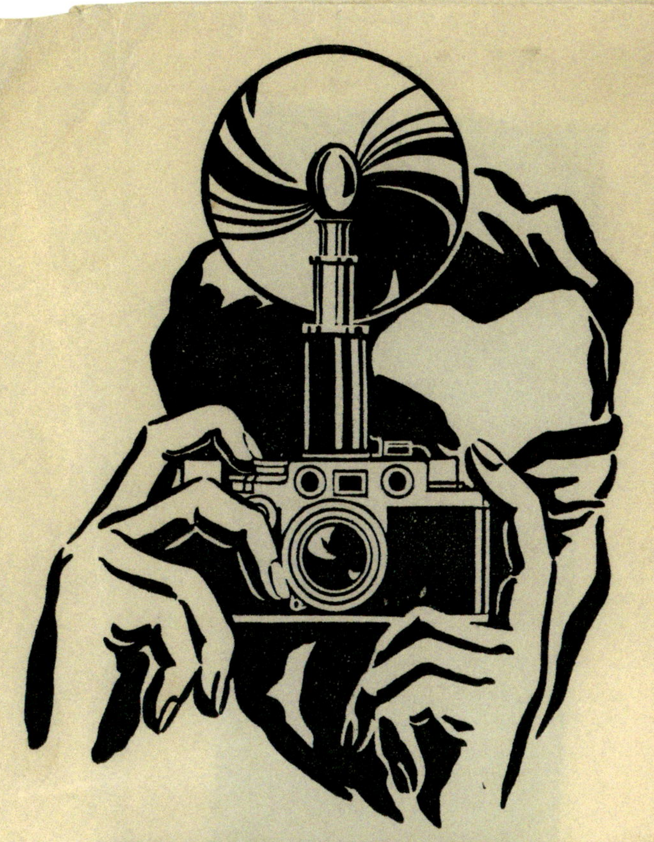

WESTMINSTER
PHOTOGRAPHIC
INCORPORATING THE LONDON CINE CAMERA CO. LTD.
LONDON AND BRIGHTON

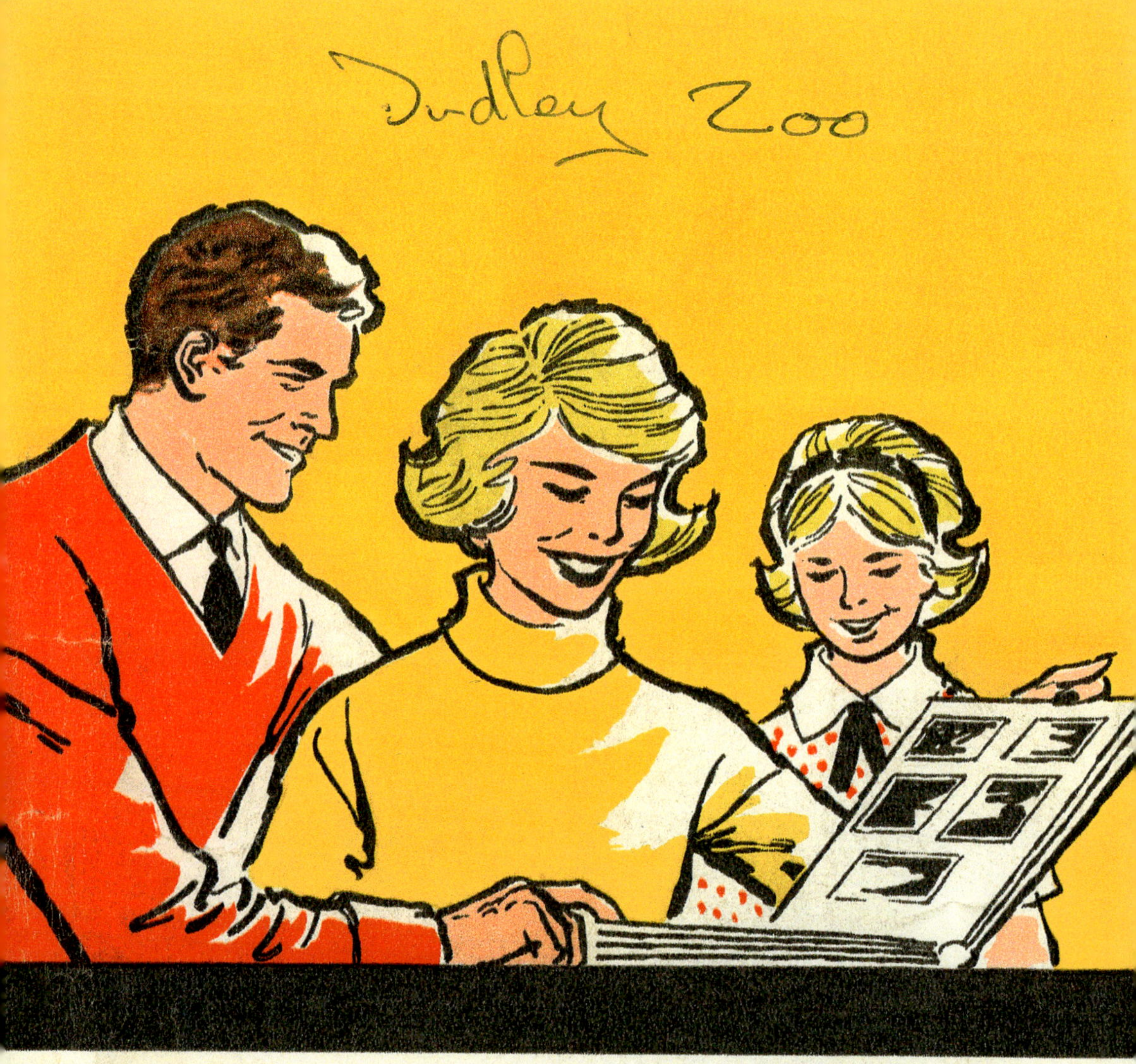

Dudley Zoo
RELOAD WITH Kodak FILM

The Family Round the Fireside

Snapshot photography was frequently reiterated as having universal appeal, but certain figures and relationships dominate on print wallets. Heterosexual couples and nuclear families are popular depictions in a form that supports and sustains social norms. Smiling couples hold photographs of themselves smiling in photographic prints in pictures-within-pictures as a form of infinite regression. The recipient of the print wallet is also implicated into these relationships: we watch the photographer, and the photographer looks back at us. Leafing through albums is commonly shown on wallets as a social practice, keeping the family together. In Kodak's red and yellow illustrated world in the 1950s, a father in a shirt, tie and crimson pullover and a mother in a canary-coloured top show their black-and-white album to their blonde daughter, clad in a red spotted dress.

The importance of photographs to romantic partners endures across time, regardless of whether the depictions show formally dressed husbands and wives in cravats and pearls, or teenage lovers in pedal pushers and loafers. In a series of wallets produced by Ilford around 1960, a young couple muse over their prints, shown freshly returned in an envelope in a sweet *mise en abyme*. She wears flat shoes and capri pants with red lips and an Alice band in her fringed auburn hair; his outfit is a casual combination, with red socks flashing between lace-ups and turn-ups. The sketchy illustration style, with visible brush strokes of loose colour exceeding its outlines, introduces a more informal era. The camera depicted in one Ilford example is the Sporti, a cheap model with an eye-level viewfinder, promoted as well-suited to new colour film. It was marketed to the young as a pocket money purchase. The couple demonstrate their youthfulness by their body language as they lean on bannisters or lounge backwards on chairs, with limbs artlessly arranged as they flick through their snaps, held as if for a game of cards.

Opposite and overleaf: The family that snaps together stays together?
Looking at prints with relatives, in an album or fresh from the wallet,
was repeatedly shown to support social bonds in the 1950s and 1960s.

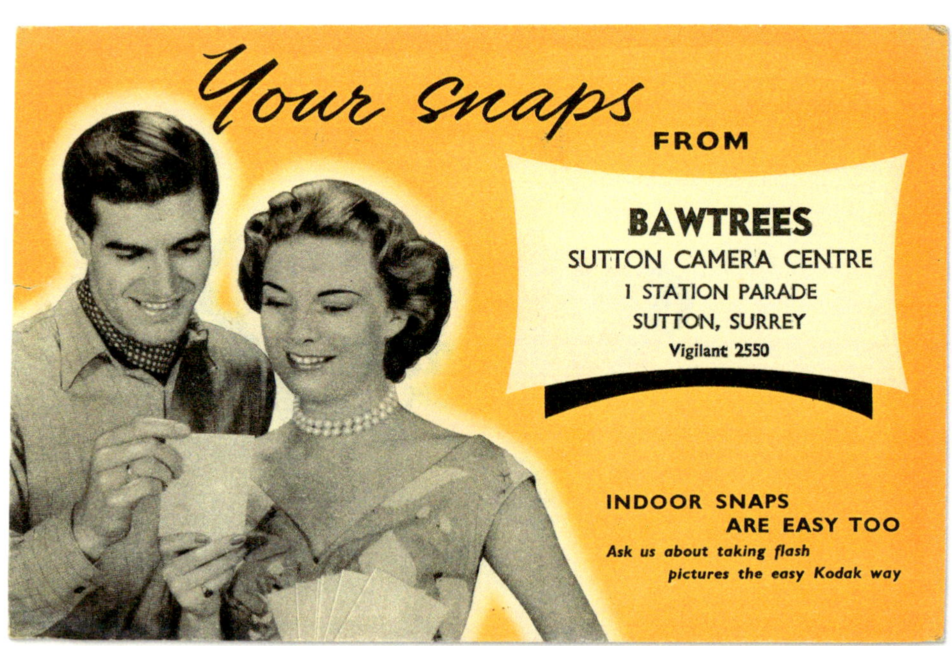

Your snaps
FROM
BAWTREES
SUTTON CAMERA CENTRE
1 STATION PARADE
SUTTON, SURREY
Vigilant 2550
INDOOR SNAPS
ARE EASY TOO
Ask us about taking flash
pictures the easy Kodak way

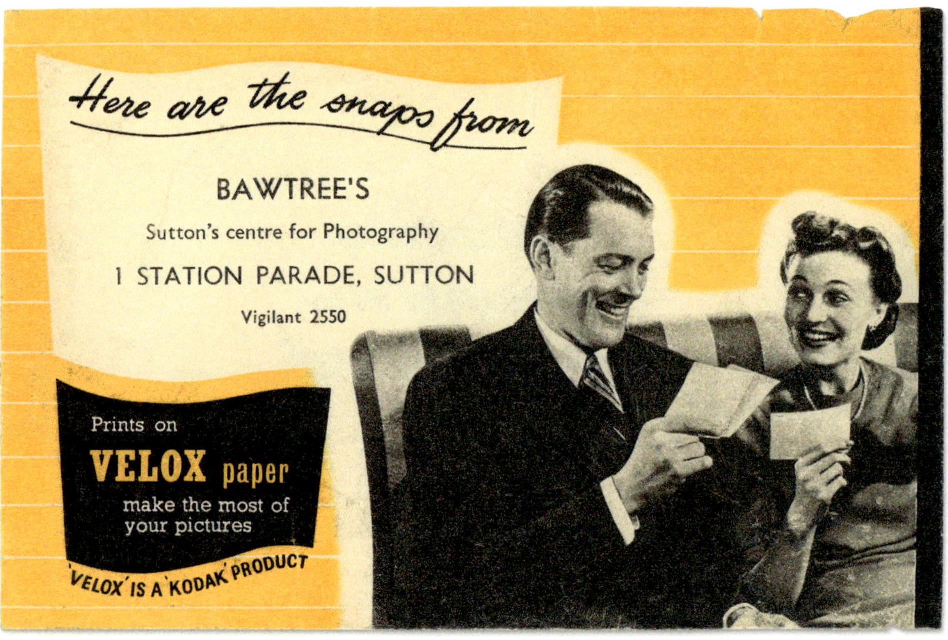

Here are the snaps from
BAWTREE'S
Sutton's centre for Photography
1 STATION PARADE, SUTTON
Vigilant 2550
Prints on
VELOX paper
make the most of
your pictures
'VELOX' IS A 'KODAK' PRODUCT

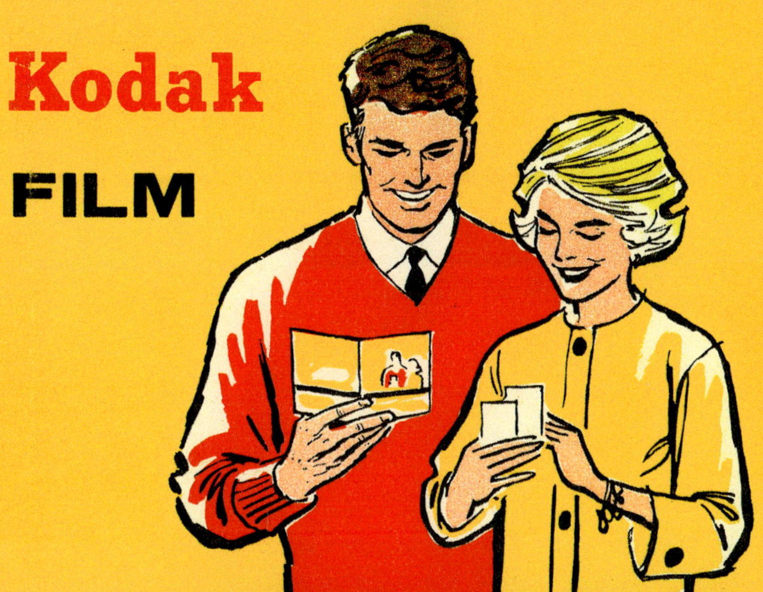

RELOAD WITH
Kodak
FILM
W. B. McCALLUM LTD.
8 SCOTT STREET
PERTH
Next G.P.O.
TEL. 24326

Print wallets offered advertising opportunities for photographic companies who promoted the latest camera, the merit of enlargements and the frames and albums to display the finished products, but the purchase of film and the use of processing services was where photography's main profit resided. Companies created personal investments with their wallets by reiterating how photography could be familial and romantic. The language they used to describe its value was affective and metaphysical. Apparently capable of stopping time and immortalising memory, print wallets asserted, 'every picture is a milestone in your life' and 'a picture is a poem without words'.

Opposite and overleaf: Ilford wallets from c.1960 show how reviewing prints with partners could be romantic. The final example includes an opened wallet lying informally at the couple's feet.

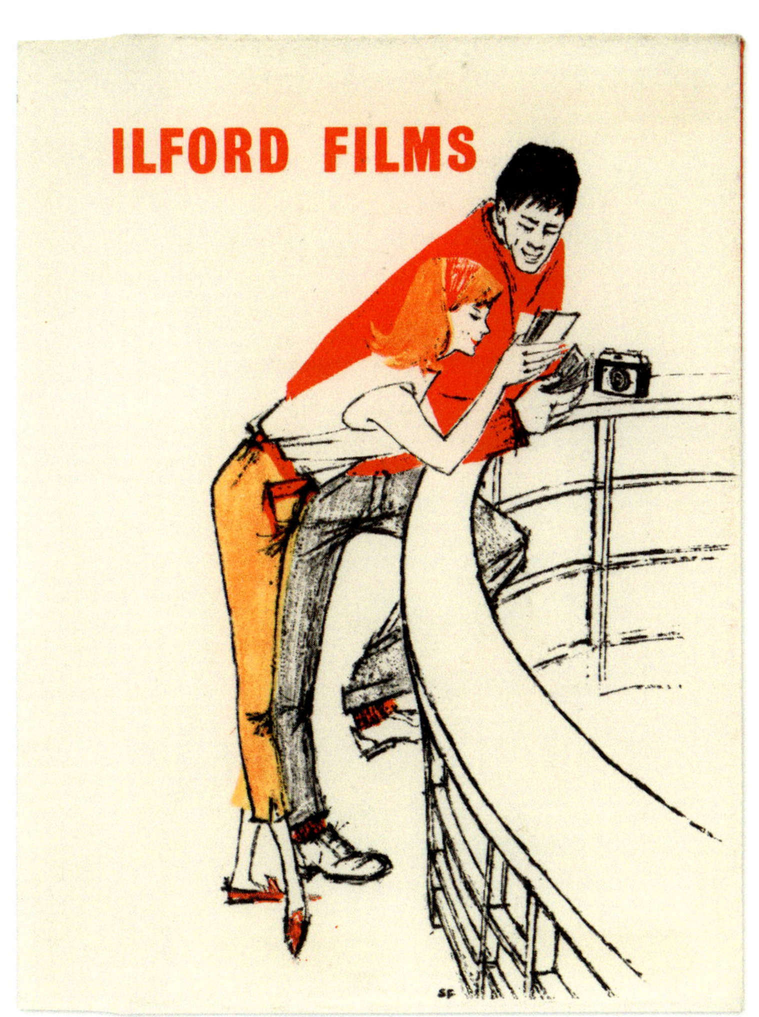
ILFORD FILMS

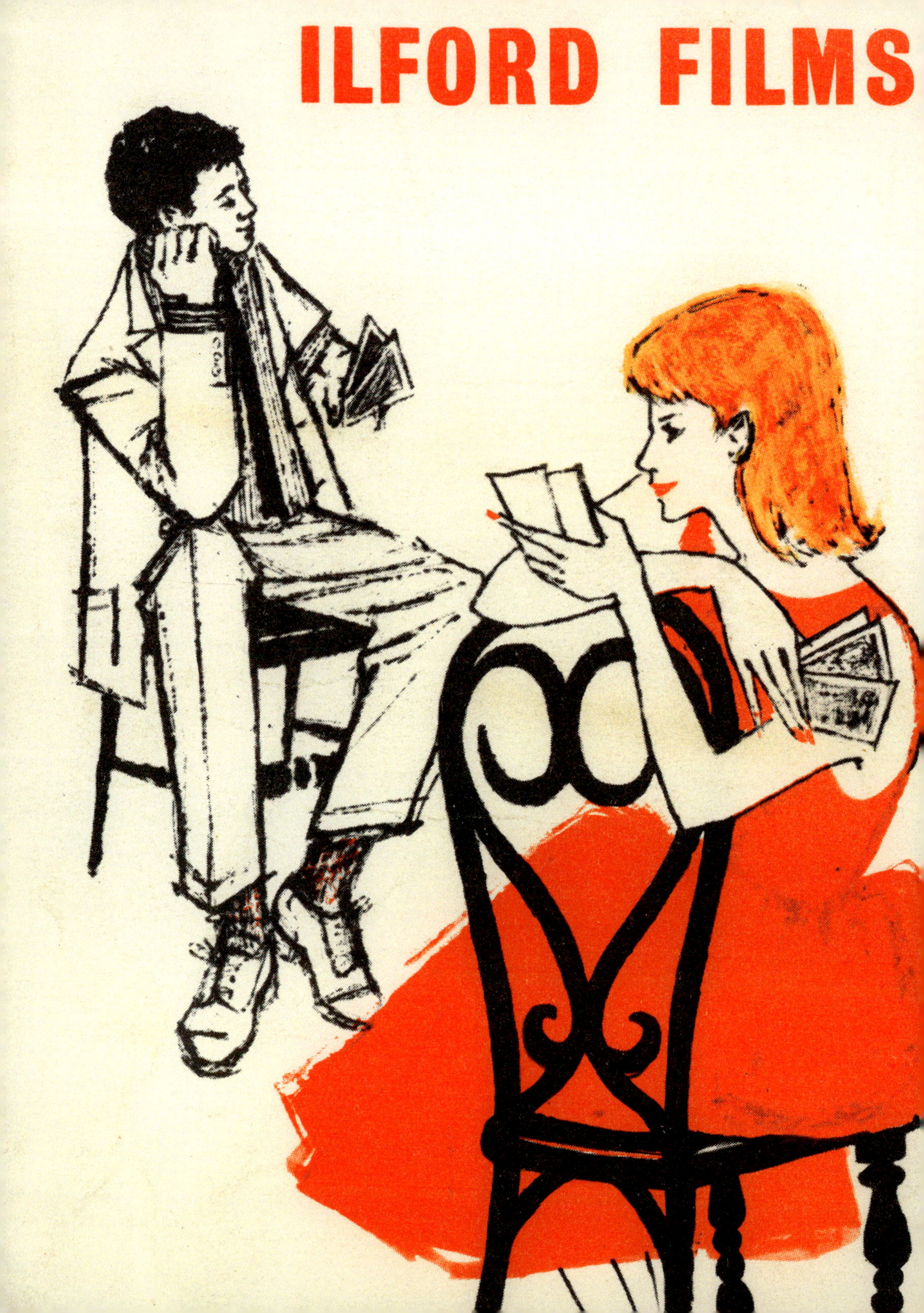
ILFORD FILMS

ILFORD FILMS

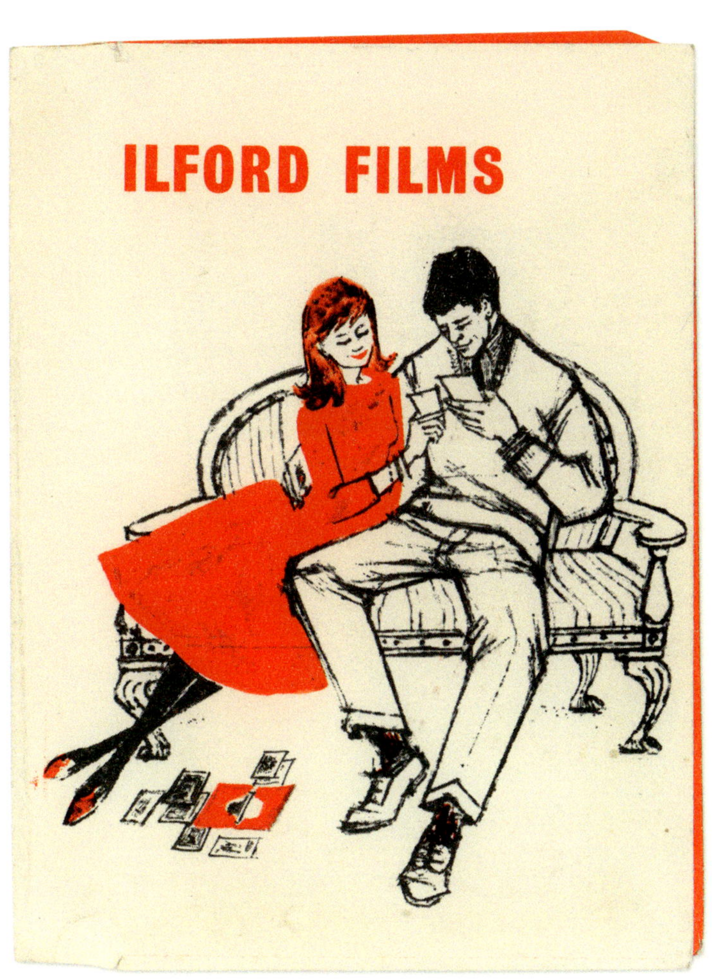

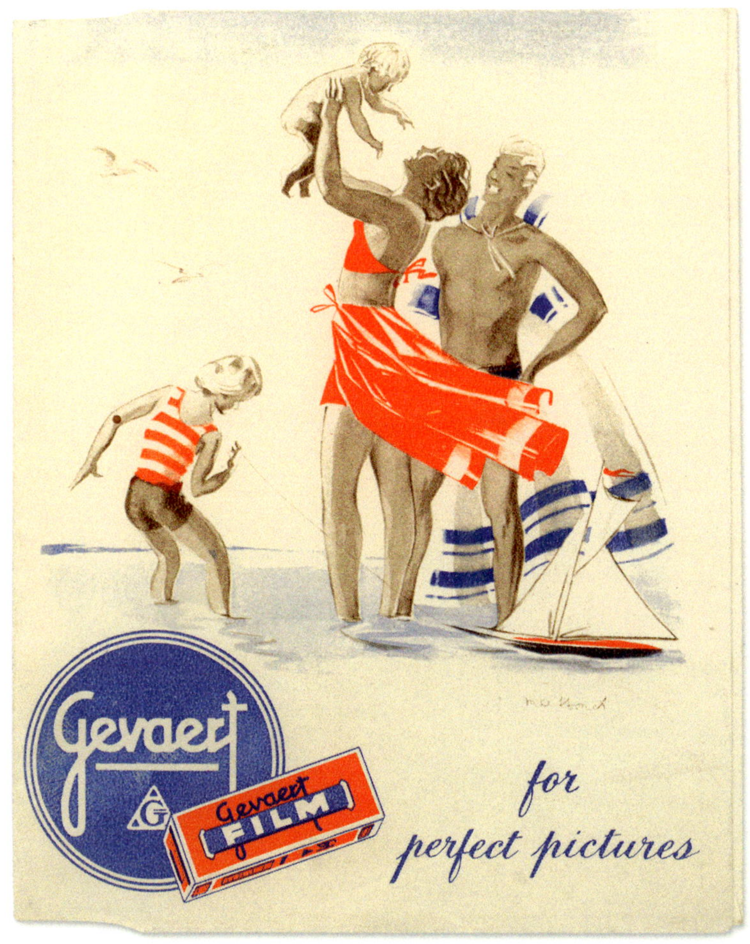

Families frolic in shallow water in mid-century wallets by German manufacturer, Gevaert. The first seems to depict idealised harmony and health. The second has a haunting gap where the child's features should appear, leaving the mood more open to interpretation.

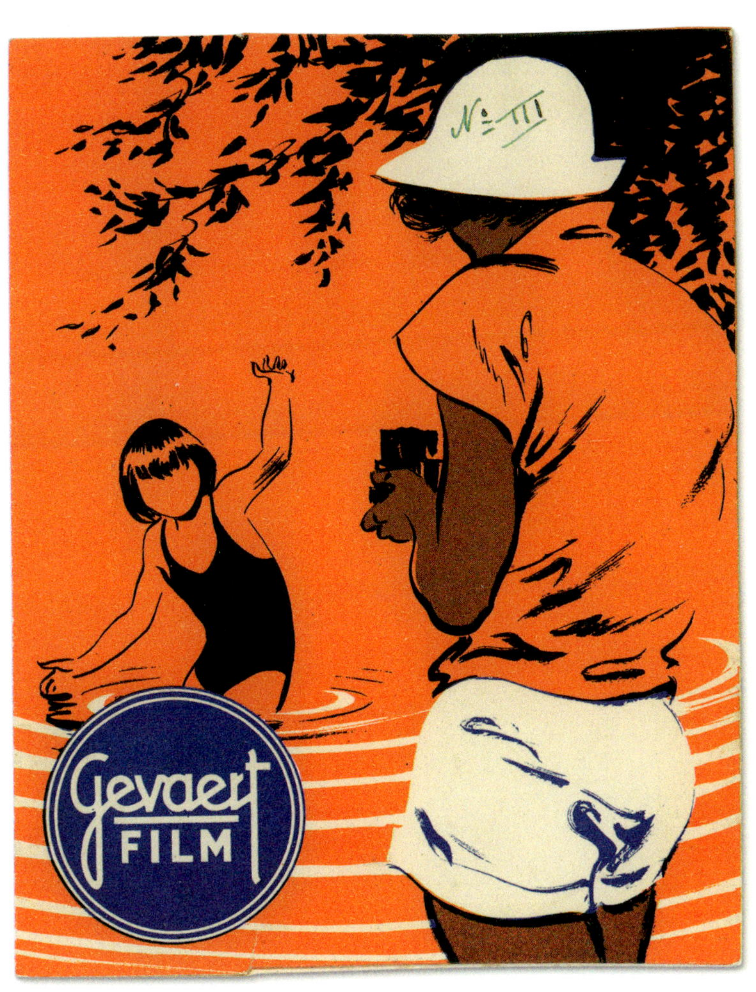
No. III
Gevaert
FILM

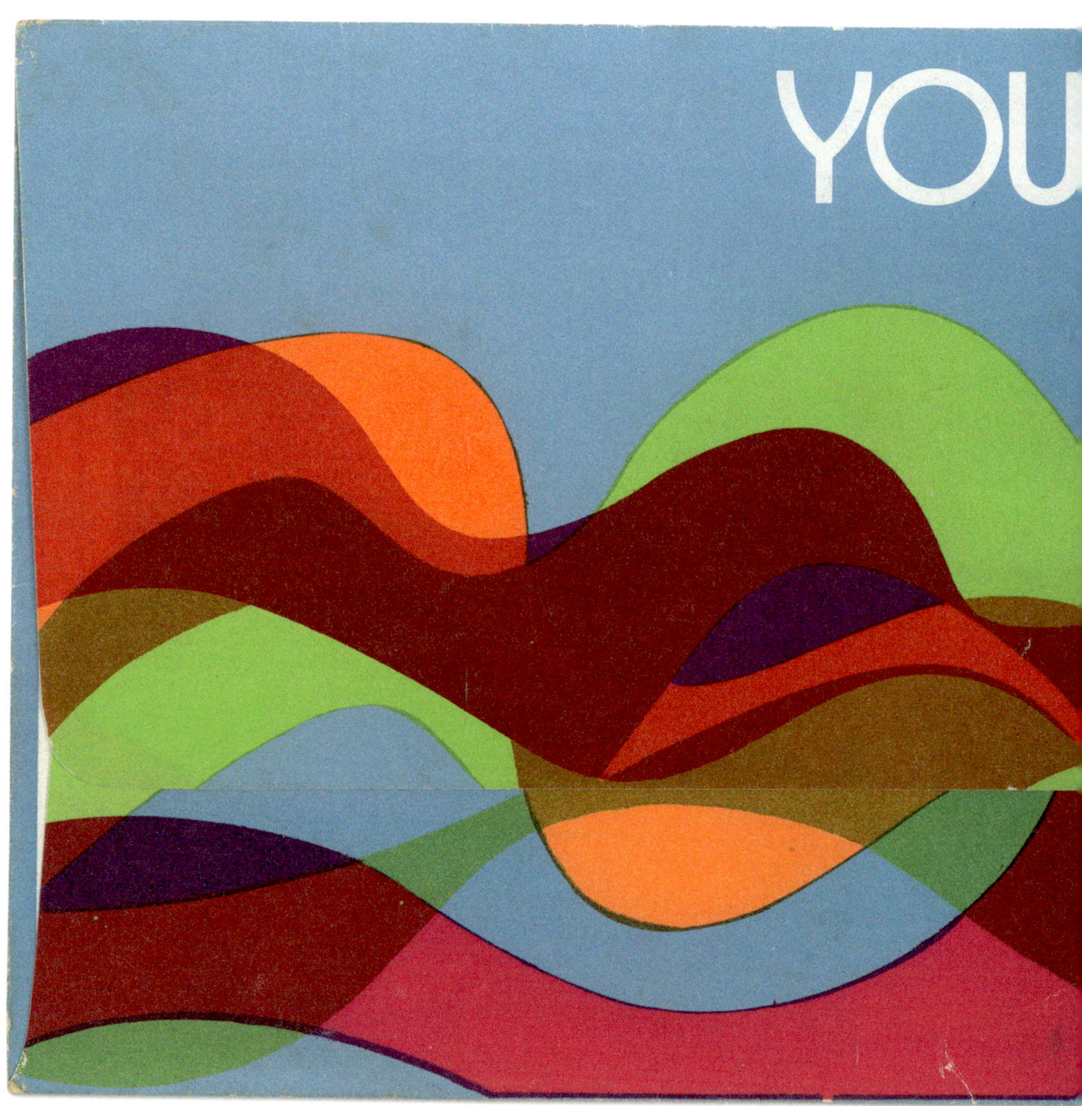
YOU

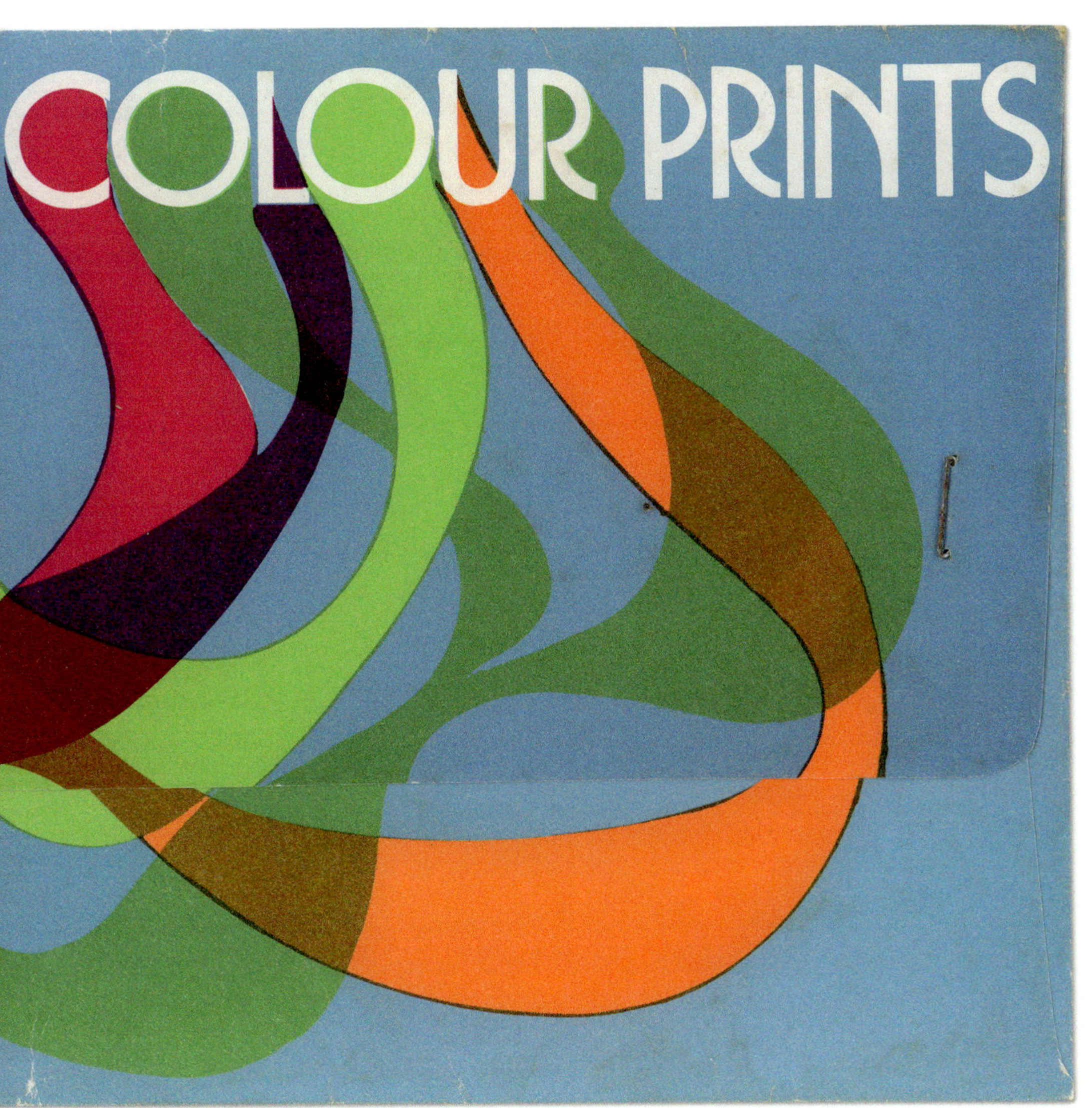

Photographic wallet designs move with the groovy times, 1970s.

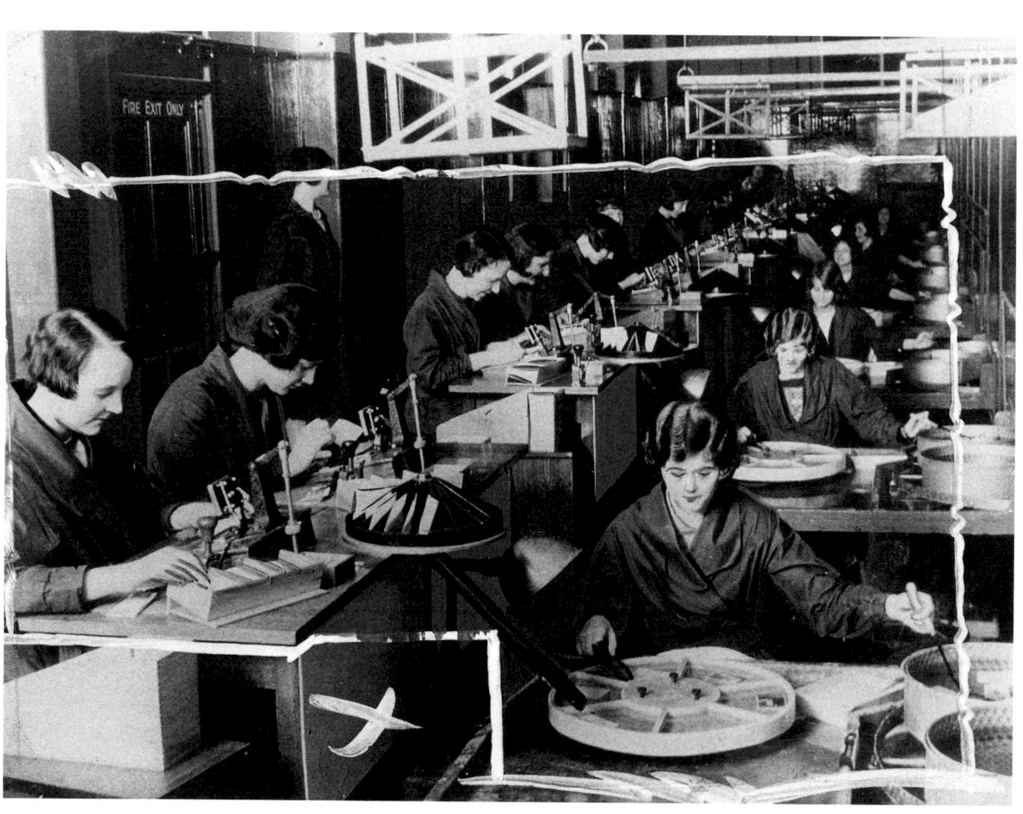

FIRE EXIT ONLY

Look with Half-Closed Eyes

When Kodak introduced its popular slogan in the late nineteenth century, 'You Press the Button, We Do the Rest', they glossed over what happened between the film being deposited for processing and the prints being returned. Kodak's service could be seen as a convenience, but it could also be a form of deskilling, mystifying photographic production for those who operate cameras. Matters passed over include industrial processes and labour practices, obscuring a body of often poorly paid workers and a highly profitable sector for its owners, in an industry that was, for much of the twentieth century in Britain, a mess of price fixing and monopolies. The designs of print wallets should be read for what they don't show as much as what they do.

In the early days of commercial processing, chemists and photographic retailers developed black and white films on their premises. A writer for Mass Observation, the British social research organisation, recalled working in his father's photography shop as a bored teenager in the 1950s:

> My first job was to take each roll and to strip the paper from the negative... Once the negative was out, it was clipped to a frame that held three such; a further clip was attached to the bottom and once I had four or five frames they were placed into a deep tank of developer and a timer set. Once the timer rang, the clips were withdrawn from the developer tank and placed into a similar fixer tank. Again the timer was set and once it went off the group of negatives were placed in yet another tank, this time of water. What fun! In high season there could be hundreds of films to process thus, so a long stint in almost complete darkness was to be looked forward to. However it was all good for the contemplation of the human condition and I thought about girls a lot.[7]

Opposite: Massed women workers develop and print negatives
in semi-darkness at the Kodak factory, in a 1932 photograph
marked up for printing in the *Daily Herald* newspaper.

Early twentieth-century photo-processing, distributed around hundreds of photographers' and chemists' back rooms, was a kind of cottage industry. As commercial processing grew in popularity, shops outsourced developing to external processors known as photo-finishers, who collected film and returned photographs in the print wallets that the retailers and manufacturers supplied. As reputations were built on speed of delivery and consistency of quality, progressive attempts were made to streamline production, but improvements were slow. In 1953, the *British Journal Photographic Almanac* surveyed American and German processing enviously, marvelling at machinery that enabled production of over 5000 prints an hour. The author hoped for further mechanisation in Britain; without it, 'it is difficult to see how… a finisher can expect to produce more prints per employee and thereby successfully combat ever-increasing costs'.[8]

Processing remained manual for the first half of the twentieth century, industry insider John Blaxland observed, because of multiple variables. Negatives varied widely in form, depending on the manufacturer. He also observed 'the absence of any kind of control being applied to developing the films; each operator had his own ideas as to what constituted a good negative'.[9] Finally, there were circulation idiosyncrasies, as customers dropped off film and picked up prints across a range of sites. Mid-century distribution was not standardised, and a variety of transport methods was at play. In 1956, processors were warned, during peak season: 'Routine collections and deliveries by messengers, on foot, cycle, motor-cycle or car, must be as regular as is humanly possible. Delayed collections upset the works, and late deliveries cause irritation to customers.'[10]

By 1960, amateur photographers had expanded enormously in number; the Photographic Information Council counted 12 million in Britain. Echoing Harold Macmillan's claim of rising national affluence, they claimed that photographers 'had never had it so good'.[11] Equipment was increasingly simple, colour photography was more accessible, and safe flash technology meant photography could become a year-round hobby, as the wallets put it, 'independent of the sun'. Flashes and snaps, as a consequence, sparkled and radiated as explosive design motifs on print wallets; living and dining rooms became backdrops as photography moved indoors. Colour's refreshing perks were first demonstrated graphically in the 1960s by multicoloured lettering and transparent shapes suggesting prisms and three-colour lenses, and later by colour photographs with the bluest of skies and eyes, dogs and babies in yellow hats and scarves, and citrus fruit in the frame.

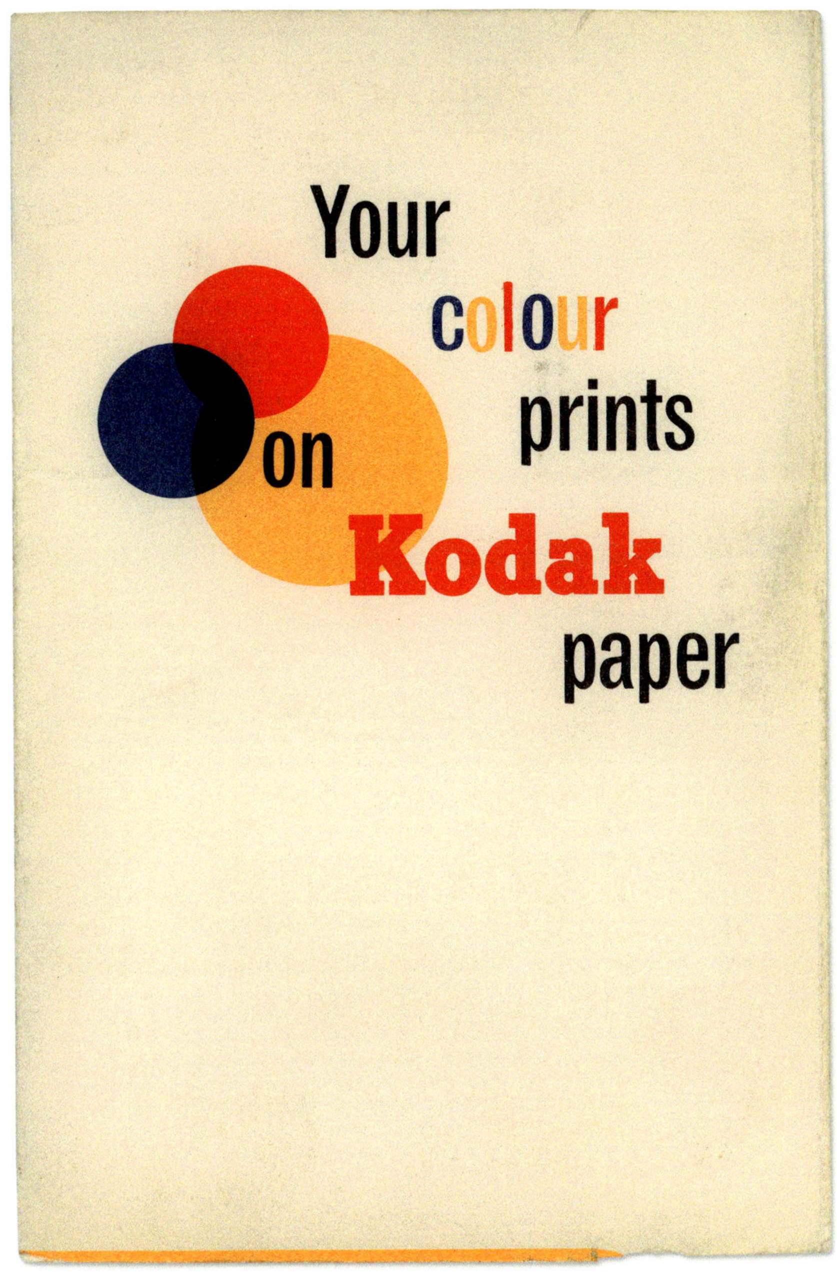

Above and overleaf: Colour and flash photography became more widespread in 1950s and 1960s Britain. Wallets promoted their potential with graphics suggesting lenses, prisms and sparks.

snap!

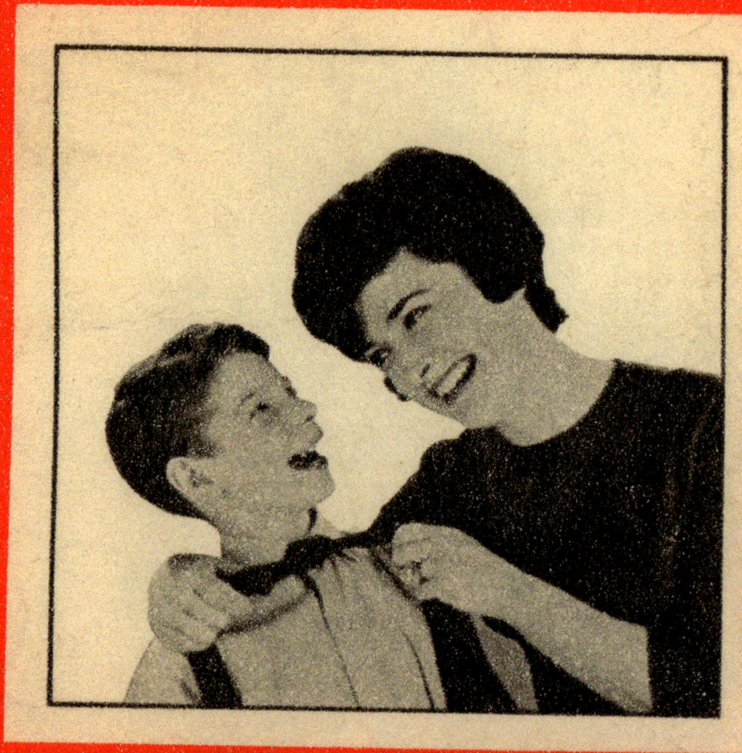

it's easy with flash

In 1964, *The Guardian* reported that photography was Britain's number one leisure pursuit and numbers were booming. As a result, production line developing became the norm: rolls of film were sequentially stripped, processed, printed, enlarged, glazed, cut and sorted. Particularly the final elements – checking that negatives matched the prints and putting both into a wallet – were often undertaken by women. Women had long been used to sell photographic products and to show it in use; they were the main users of commercial print services, and often they did the factory work behind the scenes.

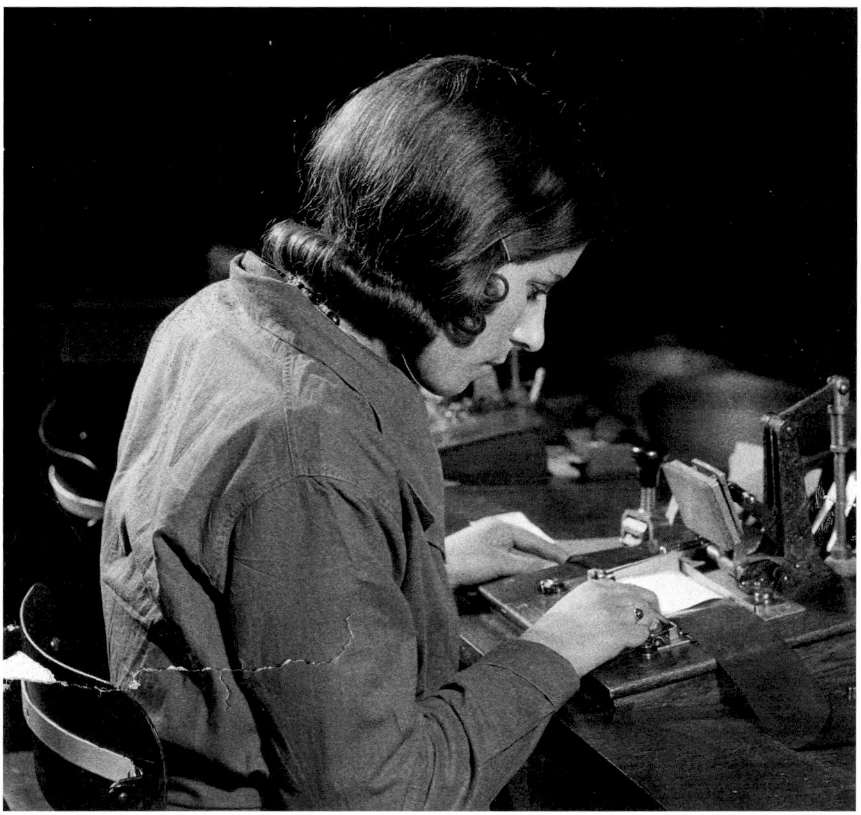

A female factory worker makes photographic prints. As photography boomed, commercial services grew. By 1932, Kodak was developing over 4 million prints a year at their Harrow factory.

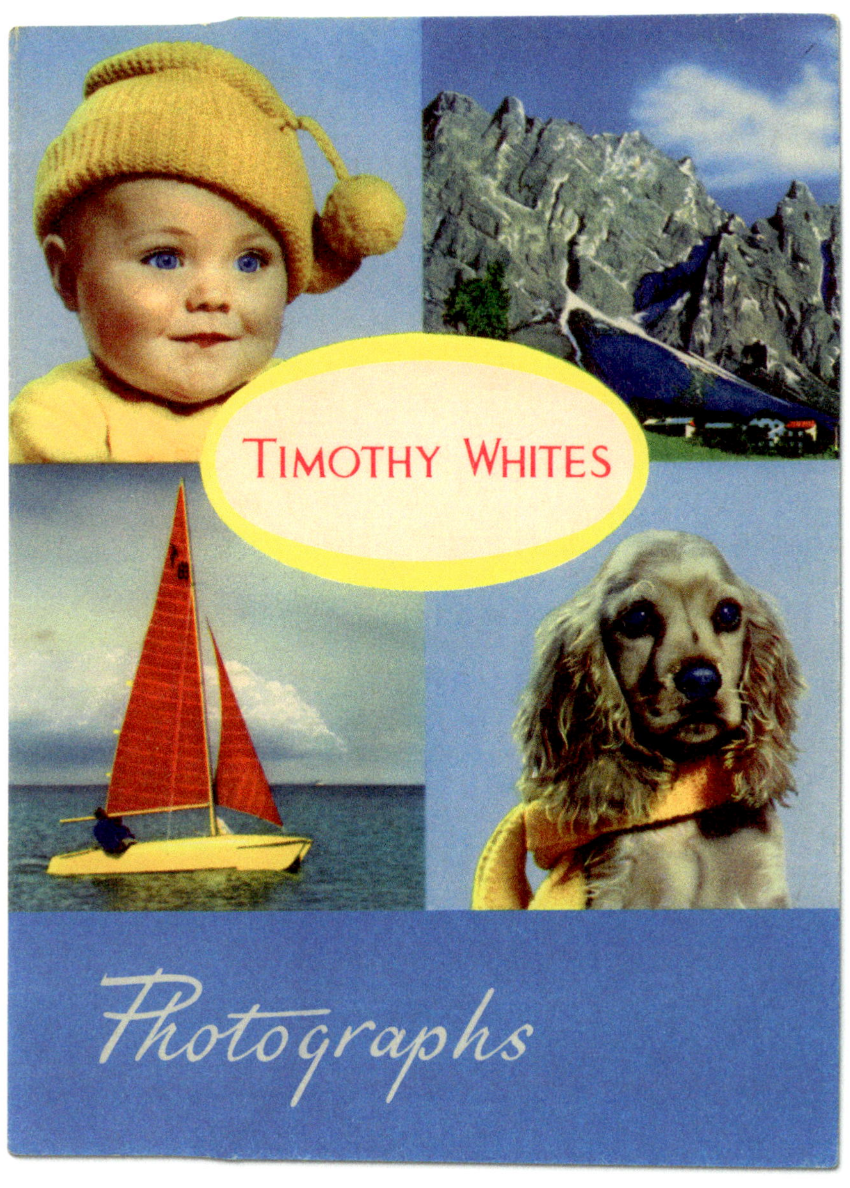

The bright possibilities of colour processing in the 1960s were
demonstrated through eye-popping photographs on wallets
where saturated primary colours abound.

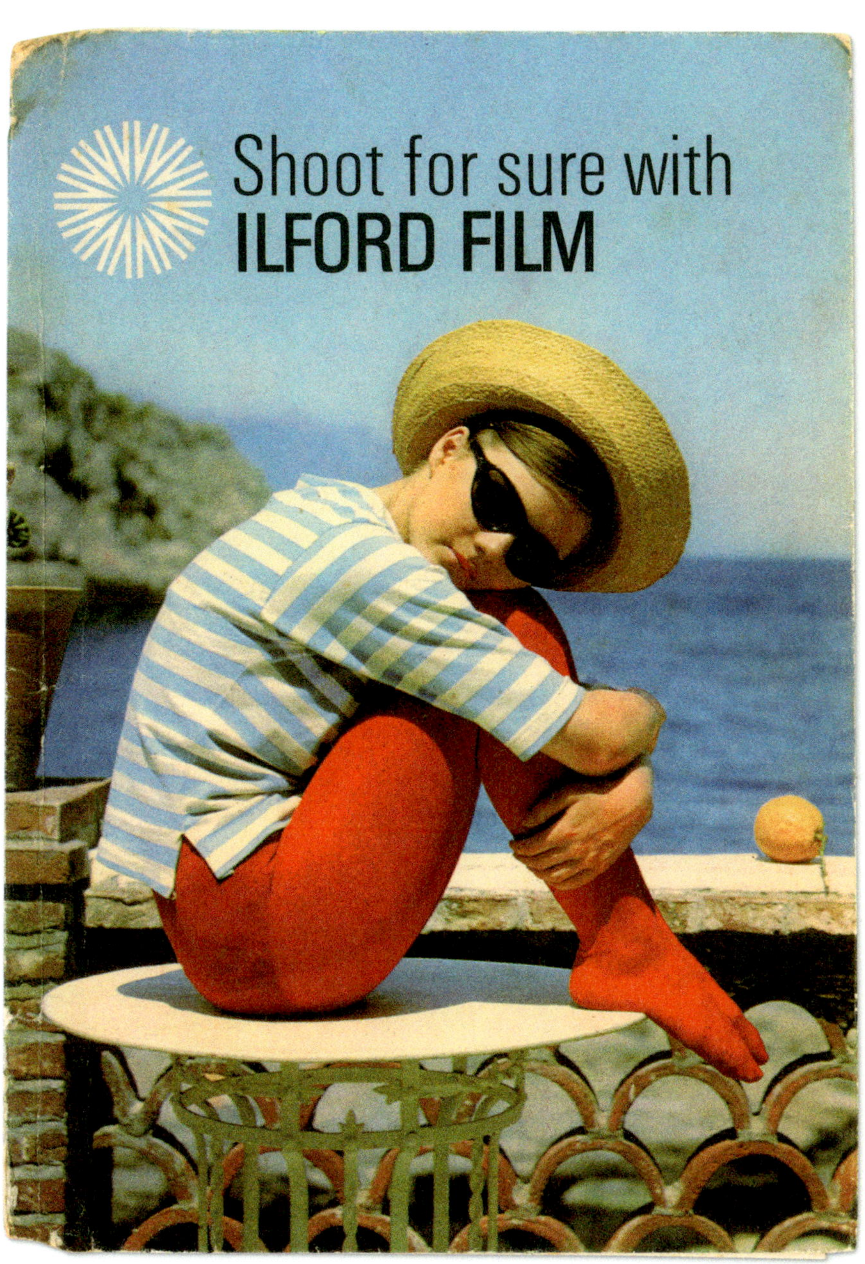
Shoot for sure with
ILFORD FILM

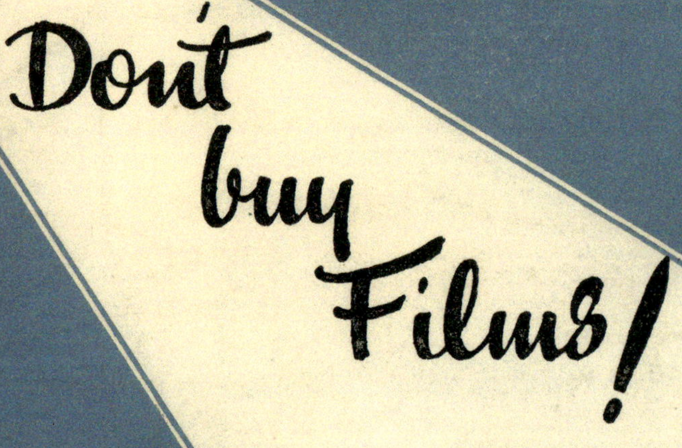

Don't buy Films!

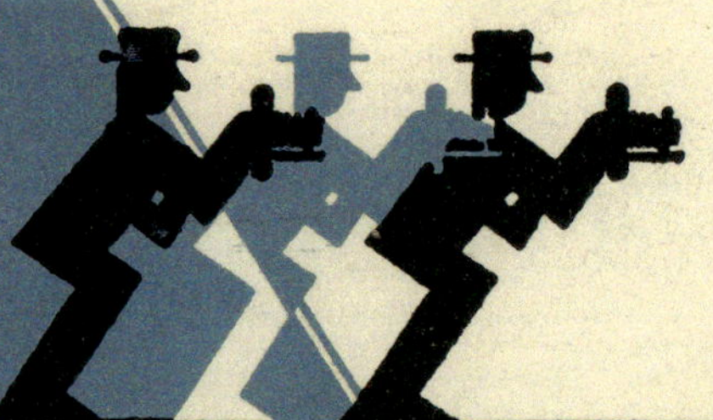

GRATISPOOL
ST. MARGARET'S PLACE · GLASGOW · C·I
MEANS FREE FILMS

A Good Print…
Unless the Conditions Are Hopelessly Bad

To maintain photographic momentum, and to expand profits, processors recognised that Britain's newly abundant cameras needed to be ever stocked with film, and that printing services needed to be as convenient as possible; mail order and free films became areas for expansion. Gratispool, established in the early 1930s in Leeds, was one of the earliest mail order operators, and the first to offer free films. They spelled out the company's principal selling point on its print wallets, splitting the name into Gratis (free) and Spool (film), under a dynamic illustrated trio of boater-wearing and camera-toting men poised in angular action. The wallets' green, blue, orange and purple iterations were linked to days of the week to make it easier for processors to identify batches when under pressure. Because the company used distinctive sized negatives, the films they supplied could only be processed by them, creating a locked consumer circuit. As they operated without high street premises, they could undercut the prices in shops. As a result, they were blacklisted by trade unions, such as the Photographic Dealers' Association and the Wholesale Photo Finishers' Association, who collectively agreed sector prices to prevent internal competition and to bargain with suppliers. Excluded from trade fairs, Gratispool advertised directly to customers via magazine advertisements and built a brisk business. When they expanded to Glasgow in 1935, they employed women as processors at a time and place when economic circumstances were dire and cheap female labour was abundant; the founders had to provide a free midday meal to stop workers keeling over from hunger.[12] The processing trade, despite the happy snappers and jolly cameras on its merchandising, was not especially delightful for its labourers, but there were major fortunes to be made at the top.

Commercial darkroom labour mostly remained in the shadows and away from public attention until some of the highest profile and most violent industrial relations disputes of the 1970s brought photo processing to light. This occurred with the 1976–78 Grunwick strikes at Willesden in northwest London, where mail order films were processed under the names BonusPrint, DoublePrint and TriplePrint. Grunwick was a portmanteau term that combined the names of its founders, Tony Grundy, George Ward and John Hickey. Established in 1965, their aim was to meet processing needs as they grew beyond the capacity of the high street. Their expanding workforce was boosted by migrant employees, particularly from Indian-born East Africans forcibly displaced by Idi Amin's regime in the early 1970s. The long hours and low pay suffered by the majority women, 80% Asian and 10% Afro-Caribbean workers who made up the 440 employees came to a head in violent clashes that highlighted the poor treatment of migrant workers as well as trade union tactics and police brutality on pickets. The dispute also impacted photo-processing: there was a postal boycott on handling their incoming films and outgoing print wallets.[13]

In the record-breaking heat of the British summer of 1976, holiday photographs proliferated like never before, but the snaps were processed in windowless buildings without air conditioning where overtime was compulsory. It was a bitter irony that photographs processed by exploited black and South Asian women who could not take time off for doctors' appointments when pregnant, and by mothers who could not maintain regular hours to attend to their children's needs, were enveloped in fantasy depictions of harmonious white families at leisure. Mail order brands circulated promotional envelopes for film processing services on an enormous scale. They slotted into magazines and newspapers and were available in sheaves in supermarkets and petrol stations. They offered free films, free duplicate prints and free postage, but their labourers often paid the price.

A 1980s print wallet by BonusPrint, one of the popular
brand names used by Grunwick Processing Laboratories.

Support the
APEX members
at GRUNWICK
on strike since Aug. 1976
for the right to belong
to a trade union!

Boycott BONUSPOOL
& TRUCOLOUR Films

Printed and published by APEX 22 Worple Road Wimbledon London SW19 4DF

Grunwick photo-processors, at the centre of disputes over exploitative labour practices, 1976–78, delivered services under various brand names, including Bonusprint, as seen in the Association of Professional, Executive, Clerical and Computer Staff (APEX) trade union campaign poster.

Overleaf: Striking Grunwick workers take to the streets in January 1977.

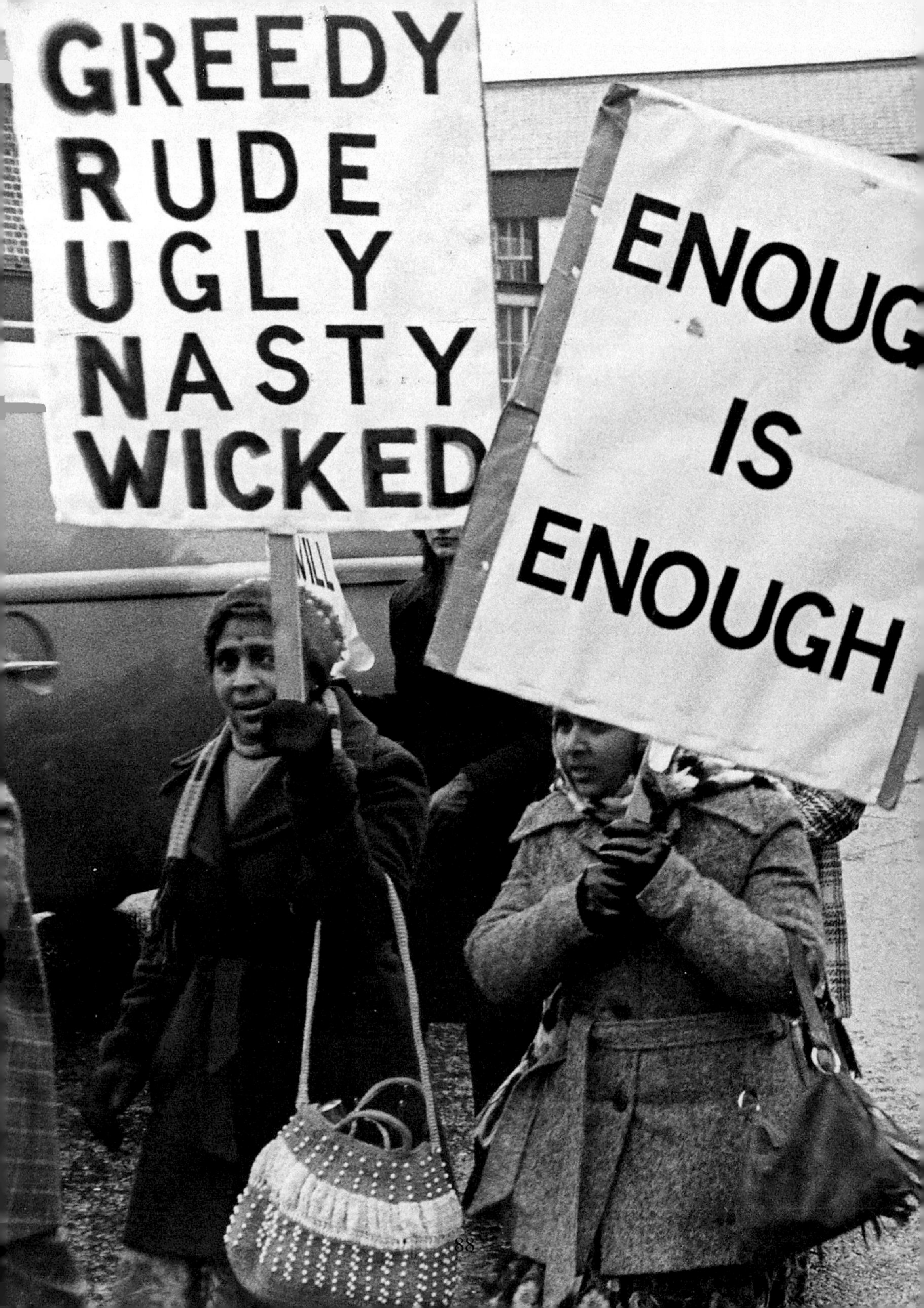
GREEDY
RUDE
UGLY
NASTY
WICKED
ENOUGH
IS
ENOUGH

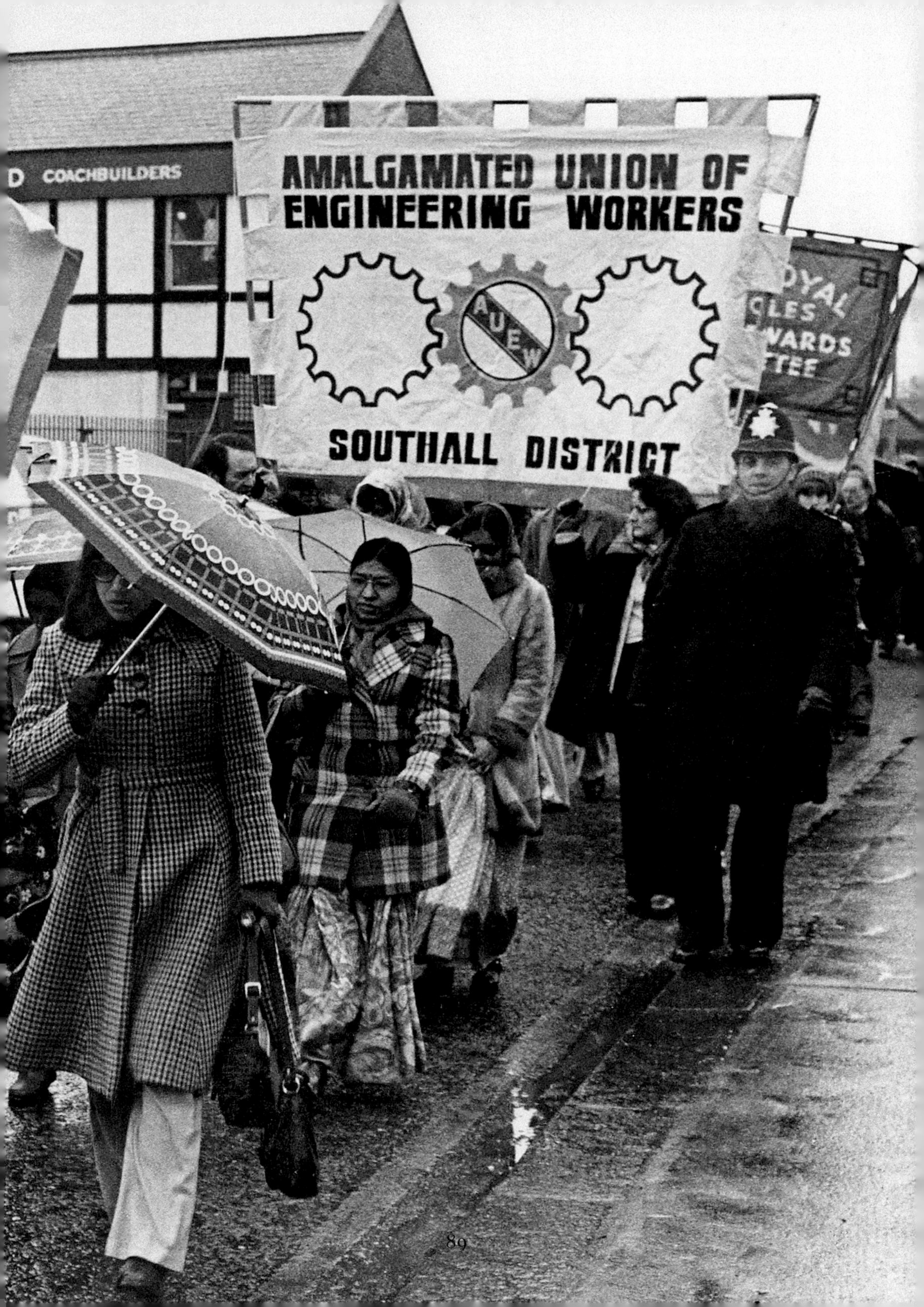

COACHBUILDERS
AMALGAMATED UNION OF
ENGINEERING WORKERS
AUEW
SOUTHALL DISTRICT
OYAL
CLES
WARDS
TTEE

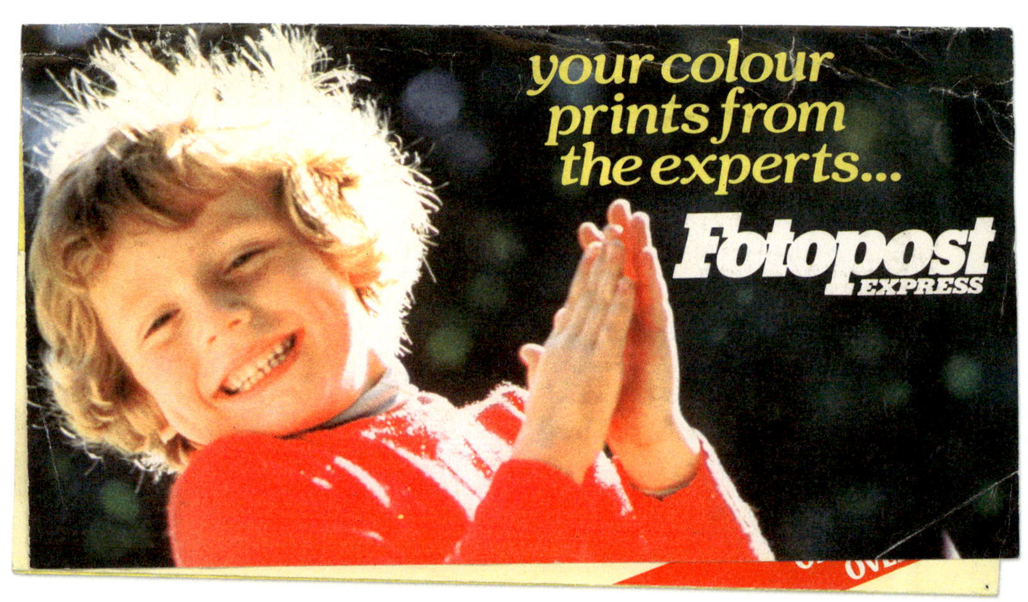
your colour
prints from
the experts...
Fotopost
EXPRESS

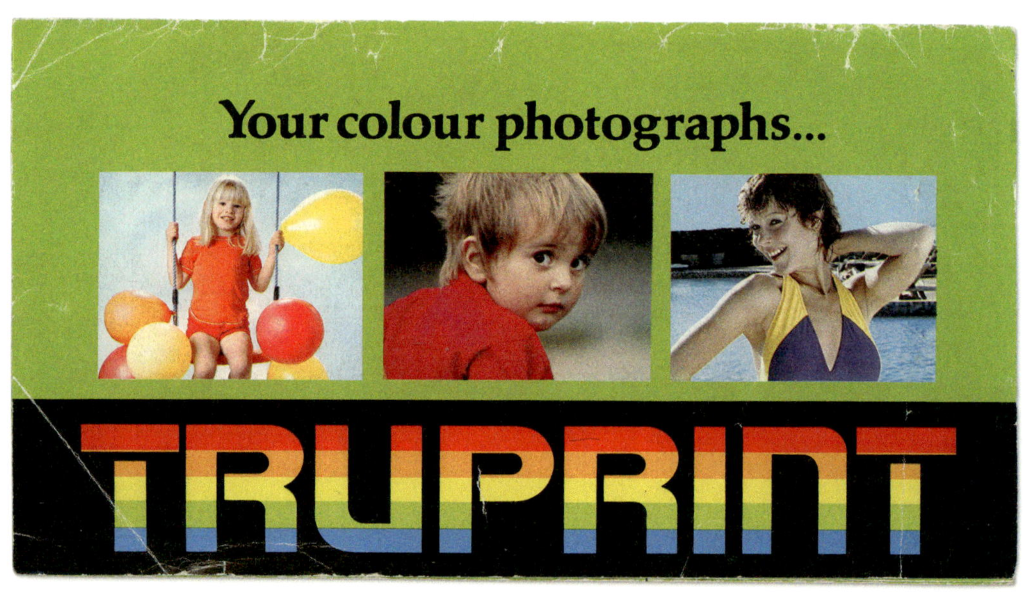
Your colour photographs...
TRUPRINT

There Is Nothing like a Good Enlargement

Migration also brought new leaders to British photo-processing. Nareshbhai Patel and his Ugandan-based brothers, for example, founded Colorama in 1972, developing practices Patel first honed in Nairobi. They began modestly by collecting unprocessed film from central London chemists, taking it to their Greenwich site by bus, and developing it through the night, ready for prints to be bussed back to retailers in the morning. Their next-day service sped up waiting times and led to major contracts with Selfridges and Dixons; within a few years Colorama was processing six million films annually. When the Daily Telegraph published its first 'Asian Rich List' in 1990, Patel featured on the cover with his Ferrari, finished in Colorama's distinctive print wallet colours of red, white and black.[14]

SupaSnaps launched in 1978, as a high street store providing photographic supplies alongside high-speed processing – firstly overnight and later one-hour – with prints returned in a bright yellow wallet to match the shop exteriors. The company's rise was rapid, expanding by 12 shops a month to over 350 premises in the mid-1980s.[15] They offered impressive sales incentives including a 'Fast or Free' guarantee if prints were not returned on time and a plastic 'Snappit' camera with every film processed. On-site mini-labs offering one-hour photo services gave high-street retailers an advantage over mail order in the 1980s when rapidity became a major selling point, reflected in the names of new providers: KwikFoto, FotoSpeed and Snappy Snaps. Increases in print dimensions were also a fresh selling point with 6x4 inch becoming the norm. Print wallets expanded accordingly, with 1980s examples three times the size of their interwar ancestors. Size mattered. 75% of the population owned a camera in the mid-1980s; there were 40 million users to entice.[16]

New promotional methods were put into action. Truprint, for example, distributed their jade green mail order envelopes through every letter box in the land, and they advertised on television. Their 1981 award-winning commercial showed subtle shifts in subject matter from popular photography's long-established themes. Instead of the traditional family break, the featured holiday showed lads on tour wearing Stetsons and

Opposite: New, large-scale mail-order photo-processing brands,
supported by nationwide mailshots and television advertising,
aimed to undercut high street prices in the 1980s.

raising pints under palm trees. To imprint the company's name in the popular imagination, instead of saying 'Cheese!', all subjects, from a bride and groom to a baby and a dog, cried 'Truprint!'[17] TV personalities too, such as Wendy Craig, star of 1970s and 1980s domestic sitcoms, lent their familiar faces to print wallets to vouch for mail order companies' trustworthiness; it remained a risk to commit a film to the post to an unknown trader rather than to hand it to a well-known, white-coated pharmacist. Photo-processing newcomers made no attempt to establish local credentials on their print wallets, as had been the norm in earlier years; instead the national scale of their operations testified to their powers. With business expanding, major supermarkets joined the ranks of photographic service providers, and wallet designs became dominated by a rainbow of brightly coloured and shouted brand names in capitals, touting for custom in a busy marketplace.

Behind the scenes, despite individual company names, by the closing decades of the twentieth century, most print services in Britain were provided by a small cluster of large-scale processors. These included Grunwick, whose fortunes flourished after the strike failed, and also Kodak, whose identity had, in fact, been concealed behind many local businesses since the late 1920s, when the company bought a majority share of around 25 British photo processors in order to keep photography afloat in lean times and to secure sales of their chemicals, papers and other apparatus. Independent processors increasingly became plankton consumed by photo-finishing predators who expanded enormously in the closing decades of the century. ColourCare International, for example, bought up smaller providers until they owned 30% of the market; at their peak they processed 28 million rolls of film per year. They also took on 60% of Boots' outsourced processing – Kodak controlled the remaining 40% – which had formerly been distributed to 60 individual businesses.[18]

None of this cut-throat capitalism was visible on the surface of print wallets, where kittens still tumbled out of baskets and children ate ice creams in blissful ignorance. But the illustrations increasingly came from picture agencies as stock photography boomed, selling promotional imagery by the yard. Model bodies on bright and glossy wallets showed off the colour processing abilities of the producers and the increasingly slick sheen of the advertising. Photographs on print wallets were always structured sales tools; they are 'fictive snapshots', as anthropologist Richard Chalfen would put it.[19] They communicate amateur photography's mood of authenticity while being carefully constructed to maximise consumers' emotional engagement. Jennifer Ransom Carter, Kodak's advertising photographer from 1970 to 1984, explained her ambition to produce 'pictures which were as close as possible to those that people would have liked to take for themselves.' The aim was 'universal appeal', she said, so that people would say, 'I want to take a picture like that...' Carter photographed holiday makers and models in Majorca: 'We aimed to tread a line between reality and unreality as we produced a professional interpretation of the family snap'.[20] In British print wallets in the later twentieth century, castles and cottages were superseded by the Eiffel Tower and Golden Gate bridge. Depicted getaways became more aspirational and international as processing businesses went global.

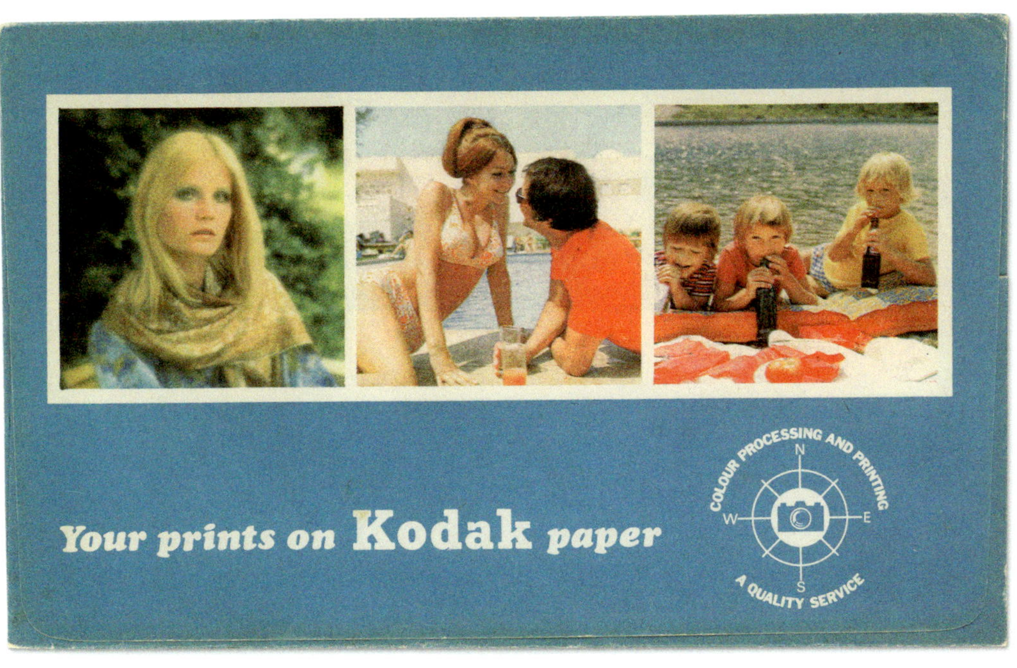

Kodak's advertising photographers in the 1970s and 1980s produced images of beautiful, youthful (and universally white) holiday makers on wallets for amateur photographers to emulate.

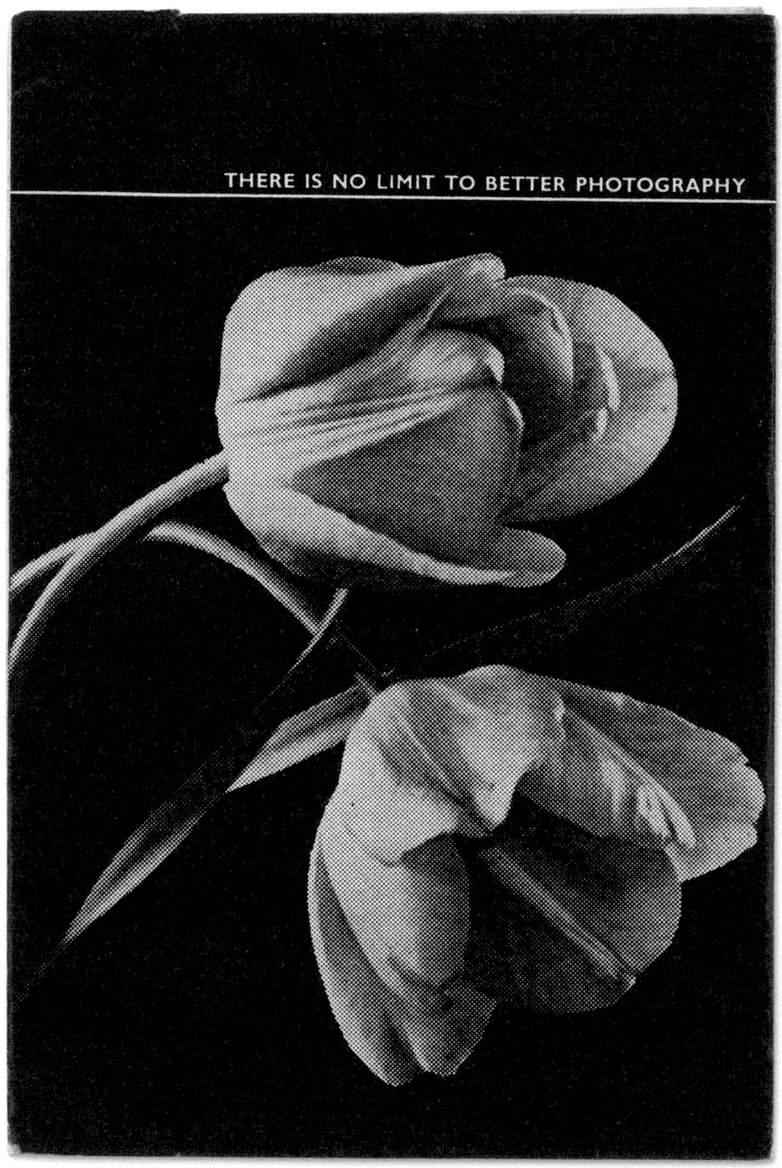

Print wallets frequently advertised dream worlds: unlimited photographic success, flowers that never fade, and memories that last forever, 1960s.

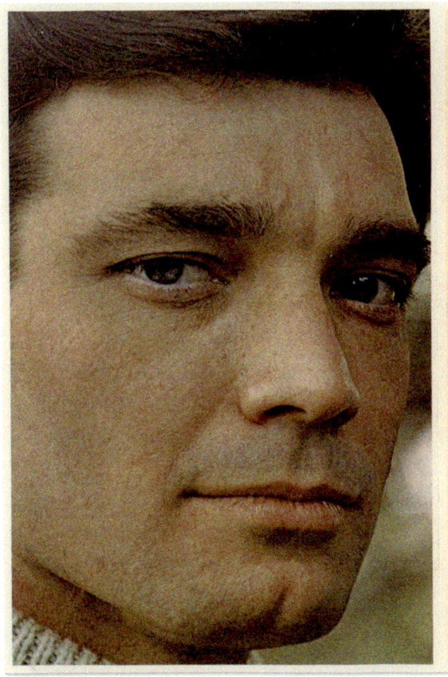

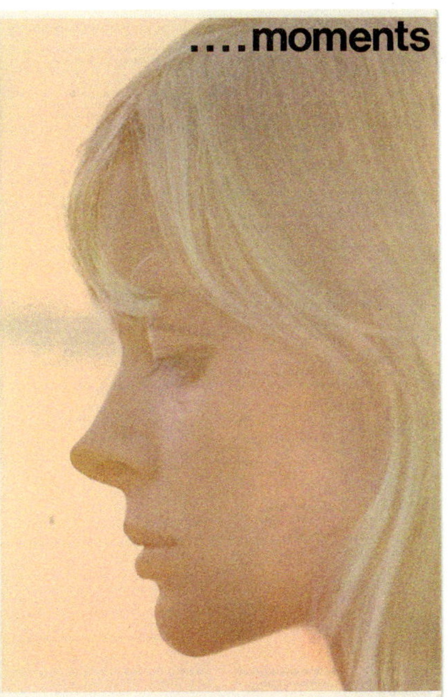
....moments

you want to remember

Life moves on. We grow a
little older. Only our memories recall those precious
moments that mean so
much, yet so easily slip
away.

Moments can last forever—
in colour.
At so little cost.

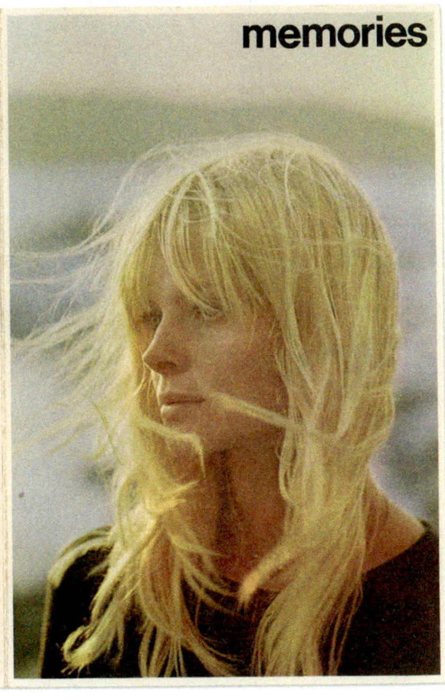
memories

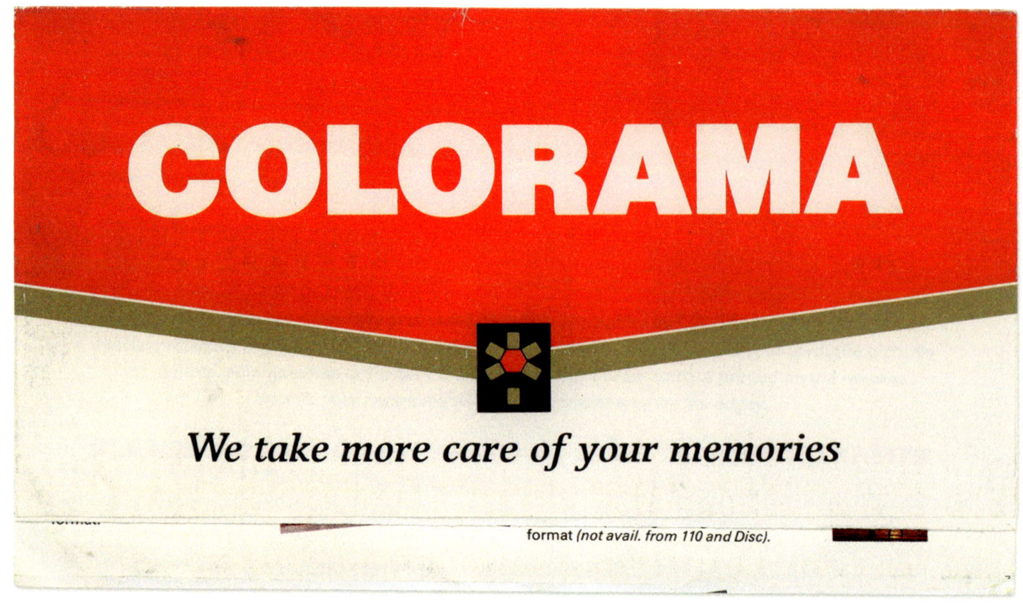

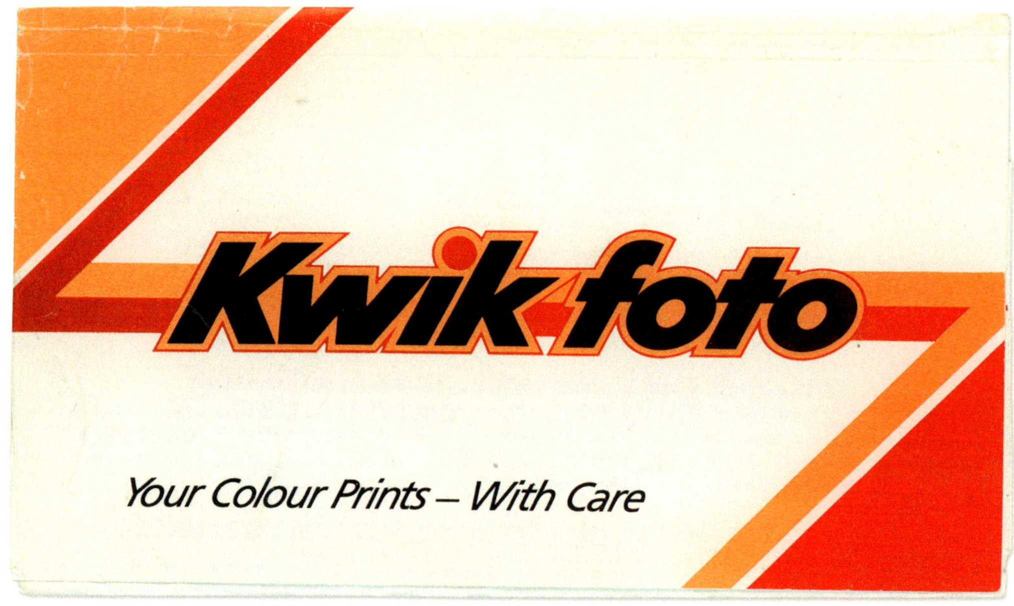

As print size expanded in the 1980s and 1990s, so too did print
wallets. Quality, reliability, speed and care were spelled out
through prominent brand names and splashy colour.

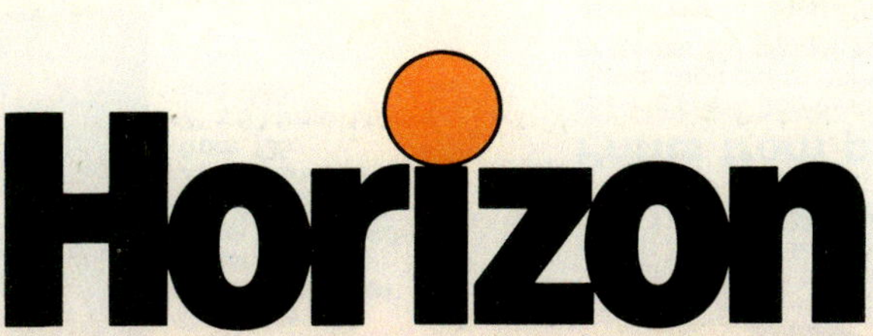

Horizon
High quality developing & printing

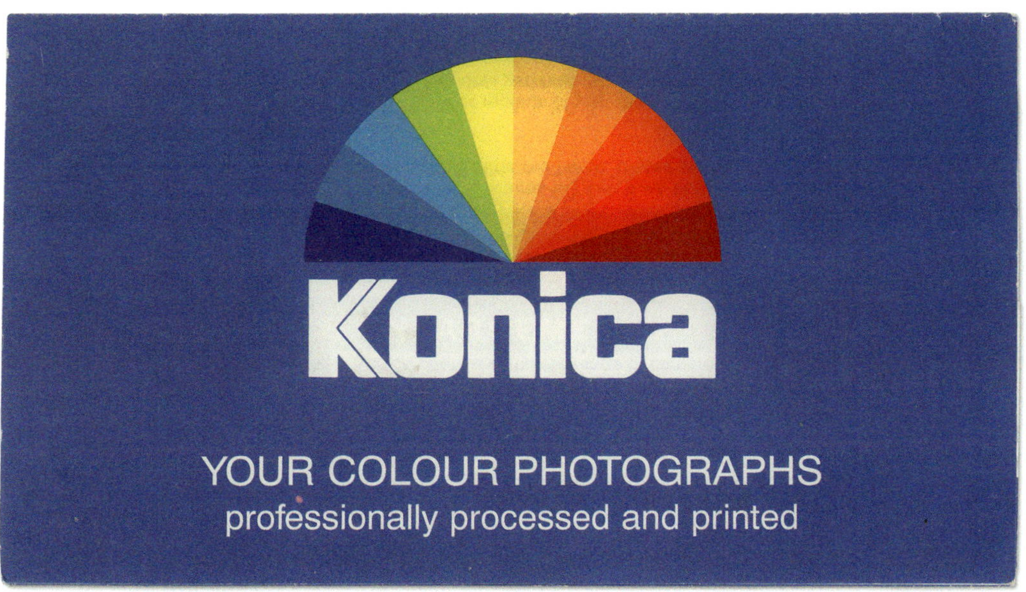

Konica
YOUR COLOUR PHOTOGRAPHS
professionally processed and printed

Hints for taking better pictures . . .

We use the most modern equipment to ensure the best possible results. We hope you are delighted with your prints which have been individually inspected by our quality control technicians. Here are a few helpful hints to improve your picture taking.

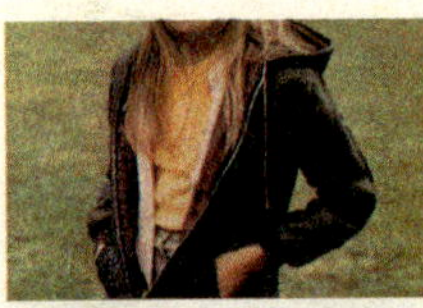

PART OF SUBJECT CUT OFF

When your negatives are printed, a narrow strip around the edge of the negatives is lost in order to prevent your pictures appearing with black edges. Take care to frame your subject centrally and ensure you are not looking through the viewfinder at an angle.

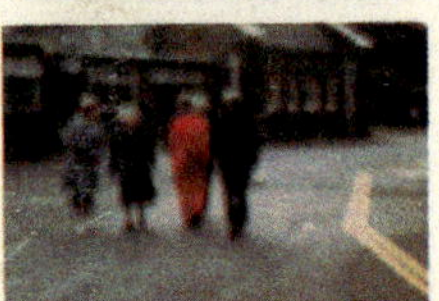

BLURRED OR OUT OF FOCUS

Fuzzy prints can be caused by camera shake, or perhaps the subject moving suddenly as you took the picture. Hold the camera steady - especially important if you have a pocket instamatic - and don't get too close to your subject.

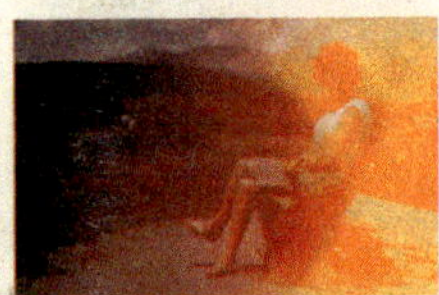

COLOUR CAST

If your prints have a colour cast, then your film may be too old or has been poorly stored. Film can deteriorate in excessive heat, dampness, or may be affected by chemical fumes during storage. Always use fresh film and have it processed quickly.

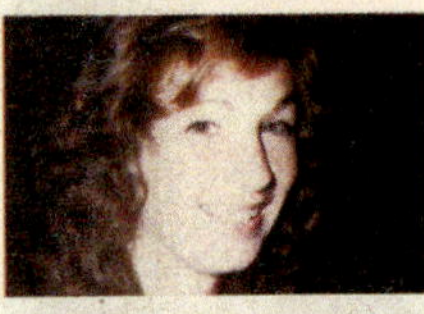

FLASH PICTURES

For best results, keep at least six feet from your subject or faces will appear washed out. Don't let your subject look directly at the camera, and beware of shiny background surfaces that will "bounce" the flash.

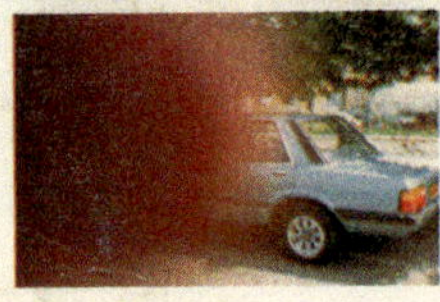

OBSTRUCTION TO LENS

Fingers, your camera case, dust or dirt, can spoil a picture when they obstruct the lens. Always ensure the lens is clean and that nothing unwanted is in the way.

from your colour processing laboratory

Druck: Kieser

DW 1677/A

Ruin Your Pictures If You Ignore This Advice

In the 1980s and 1990s, processors continued to offer technical advice on print wallets about achieving the perfect picture, but they progressed to photographic rogues' galleries of bad examples showing what-not-to-do. Decapitated children and close-ups of fingers, queasy green skies and featureless faces were used to visualise poor framing, lens obstruction, film deterioration and too much flash. Corrective interventions became more aggressive and personal as processors applied Quality Control judgement stickers directly to offending prints. Flawed family members could be slapped across the cheek with labels stating they were 'grossly overexposed' or 'too dark'. Boots offered a digital 'photo makeover' service to retouch disappointing faces.

To keep their offer fresh in the closing decades of the twentieth century, processors innovated with so-called 'companion sales', from photographic mugs and jigsaw puzzles to three-feet-high posters. By the early 1990s, wallets added the offer of duplicate photographs on CD as home computer ownership expanded. The discs contained digital copies of printed photographs but also editing software to remove red eye produced by flash and to crop unwanted elements from the frame. Photo CDs enabled consumers to email their photographs and to print them at home. In offering what they called 'the future of memories', print suppliers sowed the seed of their own demise.[21]

As digital cameras began to outsell film cameras in the 1990s, the processing industry entered a terminal decline. While some attempted to stay the course by adding digital services to their traditional repertoire, new companies moved confidently into the expanding space, bypassing film by offering prints from digital uploads or by providing online storage and sharing platforms in recognition that wet photography was drying up. Chemists were no longer logical destinations for photographic

Opposite: Processors could only do so much with fuzzy, wonky negatives. Rogues' galleries of prints on the back of wallets in the 1980s offered more realistic perspectives than the stock photos on the front.

Overleaf: Quality control stickers, applied by photo-processors in the 1980s to offending prints, added moral judgement to technical guidance.